POLICE SUICIDE

Publication Number 1092
AMERICAN SERIES
IN
BEHAVIORAL SCIENCE AND LAW

Edited by
RALPH SLOVENKO, B.E., LL.B., M.A., Ph.D.
Professor of Law and Psychiatry
Wayne State University
Law School
Detroit, Michigan

POLICE SUICIDE

Epidemic in Blue

By

JOHN M. VIOLANTI, PH.D.

Department of Criminal Justice
Rochester Institute of Technology
Rochester, New York

CHARLES C THOMAS • PUBLISHER, LTD.
Springfield • Illinois • U.S.A.

Published and Distributed Throughout the World by

CHARLES C THOMAS • PUBLISHER, LTD.
2600 South First Street
Springfield, Illinois 62794-9265

© *1996 by* CHARLES C THOMAS • PUBLISHER, LTD.
ISBN 0-398-06665-5   (cloth)
ISBN 0-398-06666-3   (paper)

Library of Congress Catalog Card Number: 96-8389

With THOMAS BOOKS *careful attention is given to all details of manufacturing
and design. It is the Publisher's desire to present books that are satisfactory as to their
physical qualities and artistic possibilities and appropriate for their particular use.*
THOMAS BOOKS *will be true to those laws of quality that assure a good name
and good will.*

Printed in the United States of America
SC-R-3

Library of Congress Cataloging-in-Publication Data

Violanti, John M.
    Police suicide : epidemic in blue / by John M. Violanti.
      p.   cm. — (American series in behavioral science and law)
    "Publication number 1092" — Ser. t.p.
    Includes bibliographical references (p.   ) and index.
    ISBN 0-398-06665-5. — ISBN 0-398-06666-3 (pbk.)
    1. Police—Suicidal behavior—United States.   2. Police—Job
stress—United States.   3. Suicide—Prevention.   I. Title.
II. Series.
HV7936.S77V56   1996
362.2'8'0883632—dc20
                                                    96-8389
                                                    CIP

To Chris, Margie, Rich, and Karen.
To survivors of police suicide.

About the Author

John M. Violanti, Ph.D., is an associate professor at the Rochester Institute of Technology (RIT), Rochester, New York, and an assistant clinical professor at the University of New York at Buffalo, Department of Social and Preventive Medicine. Professor Violanti is a retired twenty-three-year police veteran. He recently completed a study on police suicide for the National Institute of Mental Health.

FOREWORD

In this lucidly written book John M. Violanti, Ph.D., a retired 23-year police veteran and now academic researcher, provides insight into the tragic epidemic of police suicide. As Dr. Violanti writes in his introductory comments, the purpose of this book is to bring together some of the knowledge on police suicide and to introduce some promising new findings.

Police officers, we all know, are exposed daily to potential assaults and murder on the streets, yet there is another danger lurking within their own ranks: suicide. In thinking of epidemics, we think of diseases such as AIDS which ravage an entire society, but epidemics can also occur within specific groups of people. Police work is an occupation replete with psychological stress and trauma, danger, and availability of firearms. Under such conditions, an increased risk of suicide can be expected.

Indeed, police officers kill themselves more than they are killed by others. Major epidemiological studies have shown that the police suicide rate is over three times that of the general population, and rates appear to have increased over the past decade. Moreover, many police suicides are purposefully misclassified on death certificates as accidents or undetermined deaths. Suicide has an insurance dimension that could foreclose benefits for the family. Also, out of a desire to protect family members and also the department from the stigma of suicide, fellow officers at the scene of the suicide withhold information from medical examiners. Thus, the actual number of police suicides may be substantially higher than what is officially reported.

Police suicide can devastate the morale of entire agencies and leave individual officers with intense feelings of guilt, remorse, and disillusionment; many feel they should have done something to prevent the suicide. To dissuade suicide, police departments often view it as a disgraceful rather than heroic police death, and do not afford police families the support after a suicide that they would ordinarily receive in the case of the death of an officer. Dr. Violanti discusses family and peer experiences after a suicide.

Case studies are provided in several of the chapters of officers who have committed suicide. In an opening chapter, Dr. Violanti sets out case histories that illustrate risk factors common in many police suicides. Then he presents an overview of research on police suicide, including a discussion of the accuracy of official suicide rates.

In an examination of possible explanations for police suicide, Dr. Violanti points out the controversy as to whether personality or occupational elements most influence police suicide. Occupational influences include psychological stress, interpersonal and work relations, availability of firearms, alcohol use, and retirement. Personality advocates subscribe more to an individual vulnerability to these occupational factors. Dr. Violanti sets out a proposal examining the interaction of personality and environment.

Police officers generally choose police work because, like physicians, they want "to help people." The police motto is "to protect and to serve." Psychiatrists generally consider the desire to help people as being partially determined by a need to sublimate one's dependency needs by taking care of others.

Police officers are often found to be immature and have a need to sublimate conflicts with authority by becoming the authority (police officers are often characterized as "bullies"), and they are often macho (with need to prove their masculinity and adequacy). By and large, police officers walk a very narrow line between power and authority. There is an inverse relationship between authority and power—power is used when there is a failure of authority. In the words of one police officer complaining of "burnout" to Dr. Gerald Shiener, consultant to the Detroit Police Department, "It seems like no one has any respect for the uniform anymore." Another "stressed out" police officer described police work as "the human garbage collectors for the city." Another said, "We protect the rich from the poor."

According to a report in the *New York Times* (April 7, 1996), a spate of police suicides in France set off uncommon news coverage and embarrassed the government. A prominent Paris lawyer commented, "The cops are scorned by the public and badly treated by their superiors. No wonder they feel bad." To a number of young people, "les flics" (as the police are known in France) are walking emblems of the state, who are fun to taunt, insult, and, when possible, bombard with bottles and stones. Some days, police officers say, they feel surrounded by hostility. They feel they get no support or understanding from their superiors. During the days of the Soviet Union, police suicide was a very infrequent event. The police had unchallenged authority.

What about professional help for the police? Approximately 80 percent of suicides have communicated their intent by speaking of their plans or of "when I won't be around anymore." Psychiatrists find a pattern of early suicide predictors among these individuals: they become overly aggressive; they stay after work to drink with other police officers, and they use alcohol to treat sleep problems; they buy a better and more powerful pistol; they put their family in the background, in favor of their drinking buddies; they cause damage to people's property; they kill animals; and they withdraw, watching progressively more violent films.

Dr. Violanti discusses the relationship between suicide and the reluctance of police officers to see a psychiatrist. He finds that they tend not to trust police administration or mental health professionals, they tend not to be introspective, and they often internalize their frustrations and negative emotions. On psychological testing, an increased risk of suicide has been found in persons with high hostility scores. Police officers are expected to use as little force as possible, Dr. Violanti points out, and to always be "pleasant" regardless of what others did or said to them. Even though their authority is challenged, they are expected to contain their rage.

Dr. Violanti has suggestions for police suicide prevention. He discusses intervention programs and suicide awareness training for police officers. He points out that organizationally supported and confidential psychological services which officers feel they can trust are important in reducing suicide. Training in suicide awareness may also help officers to understand their own feelings and to cope with emotional adversities.

As Dr. Violanti says, the first and most important step is to recognize that the problem exists. Police suicide is a fact that can no longer be ignored. Dr. Violanti's book, while small, is a big step in recognizing and dealing with the problem.

Ralph Slovenko
Editor, *American Series in*
Behavioral Science and Law

PREFACE

There has been, indeed, an upsurge in the interest in the field of suicide prevention in the last decade. . . . On the other hand, we are still confronted with the same basic problems and the same basic challenges as we were thirty years ago. With further research in depth perhaps we may hope to find reliable diagnostic criteria and enhance the prophylaxis of suicide.

From *Suicide Among Police*
Paul Friedman (1968)

Some 27 years ago, Paul Friedman conducted one of the first studies on police suicide. The above statement which he made then still holds true today. There is, again, an upsurge of interest in the prevention of suicide among police officers, and again we are faced with challenges. Perhaps the greatest challenge is the lack of empirical, reliable evidence on police suicide. Much of the research is sporadic and focused on individual departments, and there is some evidence that police suicides are really higher than official statistics dictate. In essence, we do not know the true scope of the problem as of yet. A second challenge is the consuming denial by officers and departments that suicide is a problem. Suicide prevention is often forsaken for other training programs, and no one wants to admit that suicide may exist in epidemic proportions within their own profession.

I wrote this book to bring together some of the knowledge on police suicide and to introduce some promising new findings. I sincerely hope that this information will evoke further interest in the topic and lead towards prevention efforts. I believe that the high risk of police suicide is not a myth but an indication of the strain placed on the officer's work and life roles. I hope that this book will be just one of many resources used to help prevent these tragic deaths.

J.M.V.

ACKNOWLEDGMENTS

There are many more contributors to a book than appear on its cover. This book is result of the support of friends and colleagues. I would first like to thank Ralph Slovenko, Professor of Law and Psychiatry at Wayne State University, for his encouragement to write this book. Dr. John Vena and Dr. Jim Marshall from the University of New York at Buffalo Medical School also provided invaluable support; without their guidance, this writing would not have been possible. I also want to express my gratitude to the National Institute of Mental Health for providing funding to carry out an important study of police suicide. The grant allowed access to and development of important new information. Many thanks to the police officers and survivors of police suicide who took time to talk with me about their feelings. Lastly, I thank my family for giving up our time together to allow me to write this book. As always, the magnitude of their support cannot be expressed with mere words.

CONTENTS

POLICE SUICIDE

Chapter 1

INTRODUCTION

S ince the tragic suicides of twelve New York City police officers in one year, there has been an upsurge of interest in the prevention of suicide in policing. We are, however, faced with challenges to prevention, the greatest being the lack of empirical and reliable evidence on the topic. Much of the research is sporadic and focused on individual departments, and there is some evidence that police suicides are higher than official statistics dictate. In essence, we do not know the true scope of the problem as of yet. A second challenge is the consuming denial by officers and departments that suicide is a problem. Suicide prevention is often forsaken for operational training programs, and no one wants to admit that suicide may exist in epidemic proportions within their own profession.

I wrote this book to bring together some of the knowledge on police suicide and to introduce some promising new findings. In doing so, I hoped to clarify some issues and provide a source of information for police officers, administrators, and academic researchers. The book is divided into nine chapters, each of which discusses an important issue in police suicide. Case studies of officers who have committed suicide are included in several of the chapters.

This book first approaches the topic of police suicide from a case perspective. Suicide is unique to each victim, and these cases may provide a clearer understanding of various reasons for self-inflicted death. In Chapter 2, eighteen suicide cases are discussed within categories of common suicide risk factors including psychological difficulties, alcohol abuse, stress, and relationships.

The third chapter is an overview of research in police suicide. The chapter begins with a discussion of problems in conducting this research, such as strong denial by departments and officers that suicide is a problem and denied access by departments to important records and information. This chapter contains information on police suicide gathered by various authors from five major police departments in the United

States. This information is summarized and compared across the five departments. Also discussed is new research that suicide poses a greater risk for police officers than either homicides or accidents at work. The last part of the chapter reviews a study by the present author on the validity of police suicide rates. Findings from that study indicate that such rates are in all probability higher than officially reported.

Chapter 4 and Chapter 5 are a review of precipitating factors which may be present in police suicide. Stress in policing, as it effects officers and their families, may be one major factor. A severe form of stress, traumatic stress, appears to also be prevalent in police work and possibly plays a part in suicide. Police officers are compared to combat veterans who often experience similar aftereffects of trauma. In Chapter 5, other factors which may be related to suicide among police officers are discussed: (1) the ready access of firearms, (2) the prevalent abuse of alcohol in the profession, and (3) retirement from policing. Evidence in major studies appears to point to the availability of firearms as a potent risk factor in suicide. Police officers attach a special symbolic meaning to their firearm which, to the potential suicide victim, can make it an attractive and certainly lethal symbol of final escape. Police officers also tend to have higher rates of alcohol use than many other professions, as evidenced by survey and mortality research. Alcohol has been identified as present in many police suicide cases. Lastly, retiring from police work is difficult for many officers. The profession is close-knit and during their careers, officers are dependent on one another for support and safety. When police retire, they may feel insecure and alone as civilians. The police suicide rate among retired officers is high.

Chapter 6 is a review of theoretical concepts of police suicide, however, the development of theory on police suicide is scarce. Thus, Chapter 7 is a proposal by the present author of a new police suicide theory based on role constriction. The basis of this theory is that police officers are often constricted to the police role by organizational and peer forces and, as a result, cannot move to other life roles to deal with adverse psychological and life problems. Officers may be affected by role constriction in interactions with significant others, police peers, and society.

Chapter 8 contains information and suggestions for police suicide prevention. First addressed is the denial among police persons that suicide is a serious problem. Such denial may substantially impair efforts at prevention. Imperative in any prevention program are organizationally sponsored and confidential psychological services which officers feel they can trust. Training in suicide awareness may also help officers to understand their own feelings and to cope with emotional adversities.

The second section of the chapter includes information and research results from the recent New York City police suicide prevention program. This program is likely the first of its kind and holds promise as a model for future police suicide awareness and prevention programs. Lastly, a police suicide prevention model which includes psychological assessment, tracking high-risk officers, access to firearms, training, intervention, and research is presented.

Chapter 9 was written to make the reader aware of often forgotten survivors of police suicide. Survivors of police deaths face considerable difficulties due to the violent nature of firearm suicide, guilt, and mourning rituals such as police funerals. The police work group has the potential to provide a supportive set of conditions, but appears to abandon the suicide survivor soon after the death of the officer. It is likely that suicide is viewed as an "unheroic" death in the police milieu, and survivors must deal with their own grief as well as negative reactions of police peers, the police organization, and the public. A recently completed study by the present author found that police support can help to ameliorate psychological distress and trauma associated with an officer's death.

As is true with any problem, the first step is to recognize that it exists. With regard to police suicide, we hope that we have taken that *important* first step with this writing. I sincerely hope that information in this volume will evoke further interest in police suicide and lead towards prevention efforts.

Despite the inaccuracy of police suicide rates, even *one* police suicide is too many. The high risk of police suicide is not a myth or insignificant problem, it is an indication of the intolerable strain placed on the police officer's work and life roles. I hope this book will be one of many resources used to help prevent such tragic deaths.

Chapter 2

POLICE SUICIDE: A CASE PERSPECTIVE

This chapter provides a perspective of police suicide through the presentation of individual cases. Suicide is a personal act, brought about by conscious action. Shneidman (1985) comments that suicide is initiated by "what makes sense" to the person at the time of the suicide. Despite this individuality, classification into categories associated with suicide risk may provide some insight: psychological problems, alcohol abuse, stress and trauma, and relationship difficulties. These categories are by no means mutually exclusive. Explanations of these and other important risk factors in police suicide will be discussed in subsequent chapters.

RISK FACTOR: PSYCHOLOGICAL DIFFICULTIES

Case 1. This case involved a 35-year-old highly decorated police officer who had received seven commendations during his eleven years in the department. He hanged himself in the two-story house that he shared with his wife and child. His supervisors stated that he had been suffering from depression. He had previously attempted suicide and was being treated by department psychiatric specialists.

Case 2. A 46-year-old white male died of a self-inflicted gunshot wound to the chest in his home. He was employed for 16 years prior to his death. His entire career was spent in one district and his last several years were spent assigned as the "Officer Friendly" of that district. His last three efficiency marks were all above average, except for the last year. He committed suicide one day after his release from a psychiatric unit, where he received care for severe depression and anxiety reaction (Cronin, 1982).

Case 3. A 42-year-old African-American officer died of carbon monoxide poisoning in his garage. This officer was employed for 15 years. His disciplinary record consisted of a five-day suspension for failure to comply to department general orders relative to traffic citations and secondary employment. He received a 30-day suspension using unnecessary deadly force and bringing discredit upon the department. His efficiency marks showed a sharp drop in the last years before his death. Subject was divorced, and his ex-wife stated she divorced him due to the fact that he shot his son during a domestic disturbance, and that he also pulled a gun on her during another suspension. The ex-wife and son both related that he was very despondent over the recent divorce. The son found him in the garage with the doors closed and the key in the ignition in the "on" position. The son went to look for him because he was concerned over the father being despondent (Cronin, 1982).

Case 4. A 30-year-old, African-American male died of a self-inflicted gunshot wound to the head while at home. He was employed for three years prior to his death. His efficiency marks were all below average for the last three years; they started out low as a recruit but went even lower a year before his death. He had fifteen citizen's complaints in less than three years. The following are some of his disciplinary problems:

- reprimand—writing bad checks
- failure to return to duty
- absent without permission
- false report and conduct unbecoming an officer
- medical roll abuse lie
- excessive sick leave

At the time of his death, this officer was still married; however, the subject had been separated from his wife for six years because of incompatibility. They had three children (Cronin, 1982).

Case 5. A 34-year-old, white male died of a self-inflicted gunshot wound to the head at his home. He was employed for 12 years prior to his death. His efficiency marks were all below average and consistent for the last three years. His disciplinary record was quite extensive, with 36 documented discipline complaints. Examples were:

- improper and late relief
- used a friend's revolver for work
- failure to report back in service
- missed a court appearance
- failed to conduce investigation and submitted a false official report
- failed to report a crime
- engaged in secondary employment without permission
- discharged weapon and failure to notify desk sergeant

The police surgeon placed him on the medical disability and referred him to the psychiatric assessment board due to severe depression. He was on the medical leave for one year prior to his death. He was married and had one child at the time of his death (Cronin, 1982).

Case 6. This officer was a 49-year veteran of police work and a higher level police administrator. He went home from work one night extremely upset. He still seemed troubled the next day, and, while sitting on his bed, he fired a single shot into his head from his off-duty gun, a snub-nosed .38. He was an officer considered to have impeccable integrity. "He didn't do anything wrong himself," one senior officer said. "He was absolutely above and beyond reproach all his life."

RISK FACTOR: ALCOHOL ABUSE

Case 1. A 27-year-old white male died of a self-inflicted gunshot wound to the chest in his apartment. His efficiency marks were all about average and consistent. His medical records could not be located, but it was learned that he had been an alcoholic who had been dried out and was not drinking at the time of his death. However, he was depressed over his recent divorce (Cronin, 1982).

Case 2. A 51-year-old white male died of a self-inflicted gunshot wound to the head at home. He was employed for 27 years prior to his death. His efficiency marks were all average and consistent for the last three years. His disciplinary record included:

- false report to Communications
- failure to take a breath test
- failure to answer radio

This officer admitted himself to an alcoholic treatment center. His wife recently died of a heart attack. Upon return to work, he wrote a memo to his commander asking for help. He stated that his wife had just died and that he had been drinking after work for the last four years. He stated that since he came back to work, he had been put on afternoons and he was asking for a day assignment for several reasons. He stated that if he could work days, he could make the A.A. meetings and have a social life with his son (high school age) and other family members. He went on to say that he was very "dry" and very confused and depressed and lonely. He stated that he had to get to the A.A. meetings (Cronin, 1982).

Case 3. A 27-year-old white male died of a self-inflicted gunshot wound to the chest in his home. He was in the Marines and spent some time in Vietnam. He was employed for two years prior to his death. His efficiency ratings were below average but improving. In his short career he had received seven citizen's complaints against him. The officer had no medical file; he was on the medical only two days in 1975 for unknown reason. This officer was married and had two children. On the night of his suicide, the subject came home intoxicated and had an argument with his wife, at which point he pulled out his off-duty weapon and put the gun to his chest and told his wife, "Watch your husband shoot himself" and then pulled the trigger (Cronin, 1982).

Case 4. A 42-year-old white male died of a self-inflicted gunshot wound to the head in his home. He was employed for 13 years prior to his death. His entire career was spent as a patrolman. He had a marked decrease in his efficiency mark in the year before his death. His medical record shows several minor injuries, the last occurring during a call to a suicide where the victim inhaled carbon tetrachloride. He had also been admitted to a hospital for hypertension. The officer had been married and divorced twice and was married for the third time. He was presently having marital problems with his wife and had been drinking at the time of his death (Cronin, 1982).

Case 5. This officer had been in police work for 17 years. He was at a local bar having drinks with friends. Suddenly, he pulled out his service firearm, stuck it in his mouth, and pulled the trigger. Friends say that he was smiling at the time of the incident. The officer had a history of alcohol-related problems and was recently in the process of a divorce.

RISK FACTOR: STRESS AND TRAUMA

Case 1. This officer was 26 years of age and killed himself on Christmas day. A few hours prior to his death, he had talked another despondent person out of committing suicide. Supervisors speculated that the trauma of that event may have triggered his decision to take his own life.

Case 2. This case involved an attempted suicide of a 53-year-old officer. During his career he had witnessed considerable violence and saw fellow officers murdered in the line of duty. First, he visited the graves of the slain officers, telling them that "I was coming to meet them tomorrow." He left a note with a close friend, saying that he planned to kill himself. That evening he took a shower, put on his clothes, cleaned his gun and placed a white sheet on the floor of the basement in preparation for shooting himself in the head. His friend showed up in time to snatch the gun from his hand. Nine months later, he was dismissed from the department on a psychological disability. For the past eleven years, he has continued to recover from his ordeal and seeks to help other officers deal with the stress of police work.

Case 3. This officer was 34 years old and had been employed on the department for 13 years. One day, he drove his patrol car to police headquarters and parked in front of the building. He then exited from the vehicle, wrote "job stress" in the dirt on top of the patrol car hood, took out his service firearm and shot himself in the head. Witnesses state that he had been depressed with police work and was under considerable stress.

Case 4. This officer was 35 years old and had been in police work for eight years. He killed himself with his service firearm at home. He was recently involved in a shooting incident where his partner was killed. Peer officers said he was feeling extremely guilty and blamed himself for his partner's death. Family members stated that he would sit for hours in front of the television set and stare into space. His wife said he had been drinking heavily since the shooting and could not get it "off his mind."

RISK FACTOR: RELATIONSHIPS

Case 1. Two officers who worked together in the same precinct committed suicide. Both appeared to have succumbed to the strains of bitter disputes with their wives. One officer shot himself in the left temple as he sat alone in his house just a few days after his first anniversary on the force. Friends reported that the officer, who was on the force nine years, was very quiet and kept to himself. In contrast, the other officer who killed himself six months later had been outgoing and was always "goofing around and cracking jokes." Six months before his death this officer had promised his wife that if she went to a marriage counselor he would kill himself. During an argument with her, the officer put his unloaded off-duty revolver to his head and twice pulled the trigger. When she ignored him, he put one bullet in the chamber of his revolver and put the gun to his head. He pulled the trigger and the gun fired, sending a fatal bullet into his head.

Case 2. This 26-year-old officer had been having problems with a girlfriend. He was found dead in his automobile, a single bullet in his temple. He had recently broken up with a girlfriend, but they said he did not seem disturbed. The night of his death, he had been drinking all night with friends. When he got into a car to leave, he put his gun to his head and threatened to pull the trigger. Friends told investigators he had done the same thing several times before, and they thought he was just fooling around. One woman in the group, they said, took him seriously that night, however, and tried to grab the gun. It went off and he died.

Case 3. This case involved a suicide-homicide of a 17-year police veteran. The officer had been having recent marital problems and had been involved in an affair with another woman. At the time of the incident, he was arguing furiously with his wife. He pulled out his service firearm and shot her twice. He then placed the gun to his own temple and pulled the trigger. Witnesses state that the couple had argued often about financial and work matters.

The above cases illustrate risk factors common in many police suicides. Despite this commonality, there is no discernable police suicide profile. An examination of such cases may provide at least some insight into police suicide on the individual level.

Chapter 3

RECENT RESEARCH ON POLICE SUICIDE

Recent evidence suggests that self-inflicted deaths within the law enforcement profession are continuing an upward trend. A current study of 2,611 officers between 1980–1990 found approximately a 1.5-fold increase in the frequency of suicides over previous decades (Violanti & Vena, research in progress).

This chapter provides an overview of recent research on police suicide. The chapter begins with a discussion of problems in conducting such research, such as strong denial by departments and officers that suicide is a problem. The second section of the chapter provides a summary of suicide research in five major police departments, an assessment of the risk for suicide in officers, and epidemiological and suicide rate research. The last section concerns the inaccuracy of official police suicide rates, likely due to a desire of police peers to protect family members and the department from the stigma of suicide.

DIFFICULTIES IN RESEARCHING POLICE SUICIDE

Due to limited research in police suicide, policy for the inclusion of suicide awareness in established police training programs is scarce. Improved accuracy in suicide research may certainly have an effect on future research as well as social and public health policies. Below is a discussion of some of the difficulties in attempting to accurately study police suicide.

Loo (1986) pointed out that the variation in police suicide rates across departments may cause inaccurate statistical results. For example, a department may have no suicides in one year and perhaps one or two the next, leading to a substantial increase in suicides per 100,000 calculations. Loo suggested that researchers report modes and ranges of police suicides as well as averages.

A second problem concerns comparisons. Most findings on police suicide rates are obtained from comparisons with the *general population and not working populations.* Such comparisons may be misleading, as the general population base includes the unemployed and institutionalized mentally ill (Kramer, Pollack, Reddick, & Locke, 1972). In addition, the working population is physically and psychologically healthier than the general population, which can lead to a "healthy worker effect" bias (McMichael, 1976). A related problem is the use of death certificates as the primary source of police suicide data. Death certificate information without additional data on premeditating social and psychological factors may yield inaccurate results.

Obtaining information on suicide from police sources is difficult. Suicide is not openly discussed by police personnel; officers tend to view suicide as dishonorable to the officer and profession (Wagner & Brzeczek, 1983; Kroes, 1986; Violanti, 1994; Violanti & Vena, research in progress). Departmental statistics on police suicide are rare, and police agencies are sometimes reluctant to allow researchers access to existing data. Heiman (1977) attempted to collect data on police suicide from 23 major U.S. cities and met with discouraging results. Table 1 illustrates some typical departmental responses in his study.

According to Table 1, police departments either do not collect or are reluctant to provide information on suicide. Even the Federal Bureau of Investigation Uniform Crime Report does not provide such data. One statistic in this publication, however, noted that eight police officers died from 1981–1990 as a result of "accidental shootings, self-inflicted" (Federal Bureau of Investigation, 1990).

Another problem with studying police suicides is the lack of research across geographical and departmental variables. Most studies focus on one department and are conducted in large cities, and very little is known about suicides in small or rural departments. While epidemiological data indicates that police officers have a higher risk for suicide than the general population, such results may not be generalizable to the entire country.

An ongoing study by Langston (1995) for the National Fraternal Order of Police may help clarify the problem of cross-jurisdictional suicide research. Langston examined data from life insurance policy claims of 38,000 FOP members *nationwide* from 1992–1994. These officers were from all types and sizes of departments including urban, suburban and rural. She found that 37 percent of accidental police deaths were the result of suicide. Homicide was the second leading cause of accidental death at 26 percent, followed by motor vehicle accidents (26%) and other

Table 1
SUICIDE DATA FROM POLICE DEPARTMENTS OF 23 U.S. CITIES

City	Number Suicides	Comments
Albuquerque	0	1 former officer committed suicide
Atlanta	0	"unaware of any since 1960"
Boston	4	all by handgun
Dallas	0	no suicide in department in 20 years
Denver	unknown	no suicides in the last 80 years
Detroit	1/year	information "confidential"
Honolulu	5	
Little Rock	0	
Los Angeles	unknown	department does not keep statistics
Miami Beach	2	"during entire existence of department"
Minneapolis	2+	no accurate records
Newark	5	4 by handgun, 1 overdose
New York	74	
Philadelphia	1	data not available
Phoenix	2	1 by firearm, 1 by crash
Portland	1	5 others who had retired recently
Rochester	1	others before 1960
Salt Lake City	0	1 officer killed himself—had cancer
San Diego	2	both by handgun
St. Louis	unknown	statistics not available
Seattle	5	all by handgun
Topeka	0	
Washington, D.C.	unknown	statistics not kept
11 cities did not respond to the inquiry		

SOURCE: Heiman, M.F. (1977). Suicide among police. *American Journal of Psychiatry, 134,* 1288.

accidents (11%). Langston found that older officers committed suicide more often than younger ones, with the most suicides occurring after the age of 55. Guns were used in the majority of suicides. The average age of police suicide was 49.7 years.

POLICE DEPARTMENT CASE STUDIES

The Detroit Police Department

Danto (1978) conducted a study of twelve Detroit police suicides which occurred during 1968–1976. Three of the officers were African-American and the others were Caucasian. Seven were in their late twenties, indicating a younger average death age. Eleven of the twelve were married. Nine of the officers committed suicide at a residence. The most common method of suicide was a firearm (8 officers). In five of the cases, officers had at least one previous psychiatric consultation. Danto found that Detroit officer suicide victims had little police service time and had difficulties with departmental structure. He also found that murder followed by suicide was apparent in four of the cases:

> Murder followed by suicide was the pattern in four of the cases, but in one case, the suicide occurred one month later. In two of the cases the murder victim was the wife, in another, the victim was an ex-husband of his wife, and in the last case the victim was a bar owner with whom the officer had argued in a bar. (Danto, p. 35)

The Chicago Police Department

Cronin (1982) did an extensive study of suicides occurring from 1970–1978 in the Chicago Police Department. His findings of elevated police suicide rates were consistent with other studies. Results indicated that the average suicide rate for Chicago police over a nine-year period was higher than national rates (29.5/100,000 compared to 24.7/100,000).

Thirty-nine suicides occurred in Chicago during this ten-year study. Cronin's profile of the "average" Chicago police suicide was a Caucasian male, 42 years old, 12.5 years of education, a military veteran, and had 14.4 years of police service. Approximately 54 percent of the officers were married and 23 percent divorced at the time of the suicide. Ninety-five percent of the suicides were committed with a police service firearm. Background investigation revealed that approximately 18 percent of the officers were definitely alcoholic and 13 percent possibly alcoholic. Many of these officers had departmental discipline suspensions for alcohol-related incidents. Depression was noted in 59 percent of the cases.

Cronin also compared Chicago and Detroit police suicides and found differences in age, on-duty injury, and disciplinary actions. The average age of Chicago officer suicide was much higher (42 years of age) than Detroit (late twenties). Detroit officers were injured on duty more often (92% compared to 59%), and Chicago officers were disciplined more often (64% compared to 50%).

The Buffalo Police Department

Data from a police mortality data base of 2,611 officers spanning forty years (1950–1990) from the Buffalo, New York police department suggested that suicide rate among police officers was similar to the general United States population. However, suicide among working populations like the police (with the exception of health professionals, i.e., physicians, dentists) should be lower than the general population which includes the chronic mentally ill and unemployed (Kramer et al., 1972). When police suicides were compared with other working groups, their rate was approximately three times as great (Vena, Violanti, Marshall, & Fiedler, 1986). This study also found that Buffalo police officers were at highest risk for suicide during the 20–29 year and 40+ years of police service categories. Approximately 30 percent of officers committed suicide before age forty, 37 percent between forty and sixty, and 33 percent after the age of sixty-one. The average age of suicide was 54.2 years. Approximately 76 percent of the officers were married and 12 percent divorced or separated.

Within the last decade in Buffalo, the police suicide rate has increased from an average of one suicide every 1.75 years to one every 1.42 years (Violanti & Vena, research in progress). Table 2 provides a description of police suicide trends in Buffalo over the past 40 years.

Table 2
NUMBER AND PERCENT OF THE TOTAL NUMBER OF
SUICIDES BY POLICE OFFICERS, 1950–1990

Years	N	% Total Police Suicides	Cumulative %
1950–55	1	4.2	4.2
1956–60	6	29.2	33.3
1961–65	4	12.5	45.8
1966–69	5	20.8	66.7
1970–75	0	0	66.7
1976–80	1	4.2	70.8
1981–85	2	8.3	79.2
1986–90	5	20.8	100.0
Total	24	100%	100%

SOURCE: Violanti and Vena (research in progress).

Of interest in Table 2 were (1) the specific time periods with the highest police suicide rates and (2) the increase in police suicides over recent decades. Police suicide rates appeared to the highest during five-year intervals which represented times of significant social change. In 1956–1960, for example, there were great pressures from government and the public to professionalize the police. The years 1966–1969 was an era of turbulent social change, and the police were essentially caught in the middle between politics and law. It was a decade of job dissatisfaction and high social isolation for the police. For example, police officers were commonly referred to as "pigs" during the social unrest of the 1960s. Police officers viewed legal decisions like Miranda as restricting their ability to function effectively. The 1980s brought public dissatisfaction with police services, an increase in violent crimes, and continuing legal and social restrictions on police officers.

Thus, a pattern in decades with high police suicide rates was the pressure for change, coupled with the perception among many police officers that such change was beyond their control. One might speculate that these social change conditions were ripe for suicide, given that demands of society and police departments left few alternatives for officers.

The New York City Police Department

Within the last decade, there have been sixty-six police suicides in the New York City Police Department, twelve of which occurred in 1994. These statistics place the rate of police suicides in New York City at four times the general population (Ivanoff, 1994). Two New York City police officers have taken their lives thus far in 1995; the latest occurring in April when an officer on the force for two years shot herself after an argument with her fiance (*Law Enforcement News*, 1995). Figure 1 shows that the highest percentage of total suicides for the ten-year period was in 1994, where 18 percent (12) of suicides were committed. Second highest was 1987, where 15 percent (10) of police suicides occurred.

Interesting is the increase from one police suicide in 1992 to twelve in 1994. This trend appears to be the opposite from 1987 to 1992, where suicides decreased.

New York City police suicide data indicated a disturbing trend of considerably younger average suicide ages. The average age of suicide among New York City police was 32.7 years, in contrast to 54.2 years for Buffalo officers. Approximately 77 percent of New York City officers were less than 35 years of age, and 73 percent had less than 10 years of police service. Fifty-seven percent of these suicides were believed to be precipitated by relationship difficulties (Ivanoff, 1994).

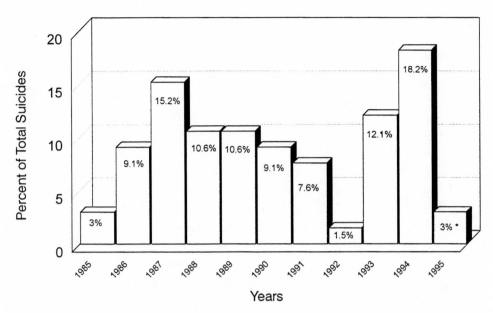

Figure 1. Police Suicide: New York City 1985–1995. Data provided by the New York City Police Foundation (1995). (*As of April, 1995.)

The Royal Canadian Mounted Police (RCMP)

Loo (1986) conducted a study of 35 RCMP officers from 1960–1983. Thirty-four were males and one was a female. The ages of officers were primarily between 20–30, with fewer suicides occurring between the ages of 40–50. Most of the officers were constables (patrol officers) and had an average length of police service of approximately 11 years. The method of suicide for 29 of the officers was by firearm, two were by hanging, one by carbon monoxide poisoning, one by vehicle crash, one by wrist slashing, and one was undocumented. Loo calculated the rate of RCMP officer at 14/100,000, which was below that of comparable Canadian rates for males in the same age range. RCMP suicides were believed to be precipitated by various factors, including psychological difficulties, job-related concerns, relationship problems, alcohol abuse, and other life strains (Loo, p. 384). Most of these officers appeared to have committed suicide in response to a life situation which they perceived as intolerable. Loo characterized their suicides as serving an "escape" function (p. 385).

A COMPARISON OF THE FIVE DEPARTMENTS

The above studies gathered data on police suicide from five departments. Although not all information was accessible or could be compared across departments, we will examine some common factors in Table 3. This strategy may help to discern patterns otherwise unnoticeable in single case analysis.

Table 3 indicates that New York City had the youngest and the Buffalo the oldest average age for suicide. Chicago had the highest number of married and divorced officers who committed suicide, while New York City officers were more likely to be single and had a higher percentage of relationship difficulties than any of the five departments. New York City officers also has the least average amount of police service time.

The highest percentage of officers across the five departments were Caucasian males. Chicago and Detroit had the most minority officers in their suicide count. It appeared that patrol officers committed suicide more often than higher ranks, with a total average of 72 percent across all five departments. The RCMP had the most suicides among higher ranks, with 46 percent of sergeants committing suicide. Suicides among ranks above sergeant were rare, with the exception of Buffalo, where 43 percent of the suicides held a detective rank.

The most common location of suicides appeared to be at residences. Chicago had the highest rate in residences, with 77 percent of officers killing themselves at home or at another's residence. It is interesting that few officers committed suicide at the work place.

Firearms were used most often to commit suicide by officers across the five departments, with an average of 87 percent of all officers using a gun. Detroit had the lowest percentage of firearm use (66%). Alcohol involvement was also present in many of the suicides, with Chicago having the highest percentage of such involvement.

While we may not be able to draw firm conclusions from this data, there are some relationships which stand out. First are age differences of suicides among the five departments. New York appeared to have the youngest and Detroit the second youngest average age of suicide. It is interesting that both New York and Detroit officers also had a high percentage of relationship problems as suicide precipitants. The inverse was true with Chicago and Buffalo officers, who were older and had a lower percentage of relationship problems. It appears that relationship difficulties and age may be related as they affect suicide in police officers.

The same type of relationship may be possible between age and psychological problems. In this case, a greater percentage of older than younger officers from Chicago and Buffalo had psychological problems prior to suicide.

Outstanding is the large percentage of police officers who use a firearm to commit suicide (an average of 87 percent across the five departments). It is possible that access to and knowledge of firearms may be an important factor in police suicide. This issue will be discussed in more detail in Chapter 5.

Although one cannot speculate beyond this data, the above studies suggest that police suicide is a complex issue. It is likely that no one factor leads to suicide in policing; it might better be considered a multidimensional phenomenon influenced by social conditions, interactional relationships, and individual dispositions.

SUICIDE RISK IN POLICE WORK: COMPARING POLICE SUICIDES, HOMICIDES, AND ACCIDENTS

Is the risk of suicide greater than other dangers related to police work? There is little empirical evidence which can answer this important question, and there are no studies comparing such risk between policing and other occupations. The National Association of Chiefs of Police recently reported that police suicides occur at a ratio of 2:1 over police homicides, but data was based on a "general estimate" of police suicides in the United States (Posner, 1995). An older study estimated the standardized suicide rate among police 20–64 years of age to be 1.75 times higher than the homicide rate (94 suicides/54 homicides). This study, however, was based primarily on analysis of death certificates and made no comparison to other occupations (Guralnick, 1963). Empirical comparisons were not made between suicides, homicides and accidents in either of these two studies.

The present author assessed the risk of suicide, homicide, and accidental deaths among 2,611 police officers and compared that risk to municipal workers (Violanti, Vena & Marshall, in press). Data was obtained from a mortality data base of municipal workers and police officers. The study used historical information as well as death certificates on each

Police Suicide

Table 3

A Comparison of Police Suicide Data Across Five Departments: 1950–1995

	New York City 1985–95 (Ivanoff, 1994) N = 66	Chicago 1970–79 (Cronin, 1982) N = 39	Buffalo 1950–90 (Violanti, 1995) N = 26	Detroit 1968–76 (Danto, 1978) N = 12	RCMP 1960–83 (Loo, 1986) N = 35	Averages*
Average age	32.7	42.3	54.2	28.0	32.0	37.8
Average Years Police Service	8.6	14.4	25.2	–	11.1	14.8
Gender (%)						
Male	90.9	100	100	100	98	97.7
Female	9.1	–	–	–	2.0	5.5
Race (%)						
Caucasian	75.8	71.8	84.0	74.0	100	81.1
African-Amer.	15.2	23.1	4.0	26.0	–	17
Hispanic	7.6	–	–	–	–	7.6
Other	1.5	5.1	–	–	–	3.3
Marital Status (%)						
Married	37.9	53.8	76.0	91.6	51.4	62.1
Single	39.4	5.1	–	8.4	24.8	19.4
Divorced	7.6	23.0	8.0	–	24.8	15.8
Separated	4.5	15.4	4.0	–	–	7.9
Widowed	–	2.6	12.0	–	–	7.3

Rank (%)					
Officer	75.8	57.1	91.6	51.4	72.1
Sergeant	12.1	–	8.4	45.7	18.4
Lieutenant	1.5	–	–	2.9	3.1
Captain	–	–	–	–	2.6
Detective	9.1	42.9	–	–	26
Method of Suicide (%)					
Firearm	93.9	96	66	82.8	86.7
Hanging	3.0	3.0	8.3	5.7	4.6
Carbon Monoxide	1.5	1.0	16.7	2.8	5
Jumped	1.5	–	–	–	1.5
Location of Suicide (%)					
Home	68	64	66	48.5	64.6
Work	14	16	–	8.5	10.2
Other	18	12	25	31.4	19.3
Unknown	–	8	9.0	11.6	9.7
Precipitant to Suicide (%)					
Psychological	4.5	26.4	33	60	40.6
Relationships	57.6	14.6	50	31.4	32.7
Unknown	37.9	59.0	–	–	35.7
Other	–	–	17	8.6	12.8
Alcohol Involvement (%)					
Yes	10.6	45	42	17.1	35.2
No	60.4	35	58	82.9	51.2
Unknown	29	20	–	–	26.1

NOTE: Blank spaces indicate variables that could not be found or matched across departments.
*Represent averages across all five departments.

case. Findings indicated that Police officers had a higher number of total suicides than municipal workers, but less total accidents, homicides and undetermined deaths.

Interesting were ratios between suicides, homicides, and accidents within police and municipal worker categories. Within the police occupation, *officers had a suicide rate of 8.3 times that of police homicide* and a *suicide rate of 3.1 times that of police accidents.* Within other municipal occupations, the suicide-homicide ratio was 3.25 and the suicide-accident ratio was .20. *When compared to municipal workers, police officers had a 53 percent increased risk of suicide over homicide, a 310 percent risk of suicide over accidents, and a 265 percent risk of suicide over homicide and accidents combined.* Overall, police officers had an increased relative risk for suicide over all types of death in comparison to municipal workers.

This study provided some evidence that police officers have an increased risk of suicide over homicides and accidents when compared to municipal workers. Suicide may thus be considered as a potentially higher risk to officers when compared to other hazards of policing and other occupations.

OTHER STUDIES ON POLICE SUICIDE

Epidemiological Research

Occupational epidemiology is the study of effect of work place exposures on the frequency of disease or injury in the work population (Checkoway, Pearce, & Crawford-Brown, 1989). Most epidemiological studies on police suicide point to a rate higher than the general population.

Guralnick (1963), in an epidemiological study completed for the Department of Health, Education and Welfare, compared death ratios of police 20–64 years of age with 130 other occupations in the United States. The author found the suicide ratio of police to be 1.8 times that of the general population. Suicides accounted for 13.8 percent of police deaths and 3 percent of deaths in all other occupations. In addition, more officers killed themselves than were killed by others.

Milham (1979) found Washington State police officers and detectives from 1950–1971 to have a suicide ratio higher than all other occupations. Police had a proportionate mortality ratio of 113, compared to a norm of

100 for all occupations. Thus, the rate of suicide among police was higher than was normally expected.

Vena, Violanti, Marshall, and Fiedler (1986) and Violanti and Vena (1986) found police to have a mortality ratio for suicide of approximately three times that of all other municipal workers.

An analysis of New York State Department of Health (1986) data for the years 1980–1981 found that police officers in New York State had an elevated ratio of suicides when compared with all other residents of the state. The mortality ratio for police was 1.79 times that of the population. The majority of police suicides occurred between the ages of 35–54.

A mortality study of police officers in Rome, Italy (Forastiere et al., 1994) found the suicide ratio among police to be 1.97 times as high as the general Italian population.

Suicide Rate Studies

Suicide rate studies are somewhat different than epidemiological studies in that they compare the rate per 100,000 of police suicides with the population. Also, rate studies do not follow a specific cohort (group of police officers and workers) through a period of time. They simply compare present suicide rates to population rates.

Nelson and Smith (1970) reported a very high suicide rate among police officers (203/100,000) according to a state of Wyoming death certificate analysis. Labovitz and Hagedorn (1971) found that police ranked second highest in suicide among 36 occupations (47.6/100,000). Heiman (1977) reported that from 1934–1939, the average Chicago police suicide rate was 48/100,000, the San Francisco rate was 51.8/100,000, the St. Louis rate 17.9/100,000, and no suicides occurred in the Denver police department.

Richard and Fell (1975), in a review of occupational health and mortality data in Tennessee, found police officers to be third highest in suicide among 130 occupations.

It also appears that police suicide may be elevated in countries other than the United States. Lester (1992) surveyed police suicide in 26 countries for the period of 1980–1989 and found that the suicide rate to be at least as high as the general male population of each country. Several countries had police suicide rates *above* the general population: Bermuda (20.75 compared to 6.9/100,000), Luxembourg (75.3 compared to 21.9/100,000), Malta (7.3 compared to 1.2/100,000), Peru (65.5 compared to 7/100,000), Poland (31.5 compared to 22.6/100,000), Puerto Rico (28.6 compared to 13.9/100,000), and Turkey (17 compared to .3/100,000). In those countries where police carried firearms regularly, firearms were the most common method of suicide. Curran, Finlay, and McGarry (1988) found police suicide rates in Northern Ireland to be very high in recent years.

In contrast to most studies, Dash and Reiser (1978) found a suicide rate lower than the general population in the Los Angeles Police department (8.1 compared to 16.7/100,000). Follow up twelve years later in this same department found that suicide rates among police officers remained lower than the general population (Josephson & Reiser, 1990). The authors noted, however, that the incidence of suicide among officers increased from 8.1/100,000 to 12/100,000 in the follow-up study.

POLICE SUICIDE RATES: FACT OR FICTION?

The validity of police suicide rates is questionable, as such suicides may be routinely misclassified as accidents or undetermined deaths (Phillips & Ruth, 1993; Aldridge & St. John, 1991; Kleck, 1988; Monk, 1987; O'Carroll, 1989; Pescosolido & Mendelsohn, 1986; Douglas, 1967; Gibbs, 1961; Barraclough, 1972; Kitsuse & Cicourel, 1963). The police officer's "working personality" (Skolnick, 1972) includes a perception of invulnerability which views suicide as disgraceful to the victim officer and profession. Police investigators at the scene of a fellow officer's suicide can readily control information to protect the victim officer and family from the stigma of suicide. In effect, the initial police investigator is the gate-keeper of information at the scene, and medical examiners may have only secondary level discretion in the classification process. A study of the Chicago Police Department by Cronin (1982) found fifteen cases of suspected suicide in the Chicago police department officially listed as "accidental gunshot wounds." Cronin comments on these findings:

> These types of cases were almost always given to the older, more experienced homicide investigators, who either out of friendship for the family, loyalty to the department, religious, or other reasons, were reluctant to classify these deaths as suicides. The old story being that they could always find a gun cleaning kit around the officer's house, and say it was an accidental discharge while cleaning his weapon. (p. 26)

If the police successfully hide a large number of suicides, artificially low rates may yield inaccurate research and discourage policy towards mental health assistance for officers. Below are case examples of probable misclassifications of police suicides.

Case 1. A police officer was found dead in bed in a rear bedroom. The officer was to report to work at 5 p.m. but failed to appear. Police arrived at the scene and received no response at the door. They forcibly entered the apartment and found the officer lying on his bed. There was a bullet wound to the left side of head, and the gun was in the officer's left hand. The officer was lying on his back in bed. The apartment was locked, there was no sign of forcible entry, and the officer's own gun was found in his hand. Cause of death: *Undetermined.*

Case 2. An off-duty police officer was at a tavern drinking with friends. Suddenly, the officer took out his revolver, placed it in his mouth and pulled the trigger. The bullet went through roof of his mouth and exited on top of his head. Witnesses state that he was not "fooling around" with his gun and was not exhibiting careless behavior. Evidence was presented that the officer exhibited full intent to shot himself and the discharge of the gun was not accidental. Cause of death: *Undetermined/accidental.*

Case 3. A police officer was found in the police locker room by someone who heard a shot and went in to investigate. The officer was found slumped over in a prone position on the locker room floor. A gunshot wound was noted in the officer's right temple area and his gun was found on the floor. The death was ruled as undetermined because it was theorized by police investigators that his gun may have "fallen from the top of his locker" and discharged a round into his temple. The victim had recently been a patient at Veterans hospital and was reported to be in ill health. Five spent rounds were found at the scene. Cause of death: *Undetermined/accidental.*

Case 4. Police officer victim was reported to be depressed and in ill health. He was found sitting in an easy chair in a back bedroom with a gunshot wound in his left temple. The bullet exited through the right temple. The officer's revolver was found beside the body. Cause of death: *Undetermined.*

All four of these cases involved gunshot wounds to the temple area of the head. This type of wound is commonly found in suicides, yet these police deaths were classified as undetermined.

An Attempt to Determine the Accuracy of Police Suicide Rates

Other than anecdotal information, there is no scientific evidence of police suicide misclassification. In an attempt to clarify this situation, this author conducted a study to test how well "officially" *reported* police suicide rates like those in the above cases represented the *actual* police suicide rate. Specifically, the study addressed how sensitive official rates are in detecting true police suicides. In addition, the study compared the accuracy of police suicide rates with rates of other municipal workers (Violanti, Vena, Marshall, & Petralia, in press).

The study was conducted on a large epidemiological data base of 11,760 city workers, which included police officers and persons in other city jobs (Vena et al., 1986). Vital status and death classifications were obtained for police officers who worked a minimum of five years in their specific occupational group between the years 1950–1990. Sources of vital status follow up included benefit and pension programs, the state retirement system, voter registration records, the department of motor vehicles, the social security administration, city directories, obituaries, and the National Death Index Data Base. Information was located on 98 percent of officers and other workers.

"True" Suicide Case Identification

Ideally, the validity of police suicides should be measured against some "gold standard" of suicide (Holding & Barraclough, 1978; Kirsher, Nelson, & Burdo, 1985; Litman, Curphey, Shneidman, Farberow, & Tabachnick, 1963; McCarthy & Walsh, 1975; Moyer, Boyle, & Pollock, 1989; O'Carroll, 1989; Phillips & Ruth, 1993). Since no such definitive standard exists for police, we used an alternate strategy to establish a validity comparison base. First, deaths listed in the data base as suicides, accidents, or undetermined causes were collected. Accident and undetermined death classifications were selected in addition to suicides because suicide has been shown to be systematically misreported within these categories (Barraclough, 1972; Barraclough, 1974; Douglas, 1967; Kitsuse & Cicourel, 1963; O'Carroll, 1989; Pescosolido & Mendelsohn, 1986). One hundred and thirty-eight complete cases resulted: 49 police officers and 89 municipal workers. Information on each of these persons was compiled from death certificates, medical examiner reports, autopsies, police investigative reports, newspaper accounts, and obituaries and given to a panel of experts to make independent re-evaluations of official death classifications. The panel consisted of one chief and two associate county-level medical examiners, all of whom had M.D. degrees, investigated at least 300 cases per year, and were employed an average of 30.6 years. Medical examiners were blinded to identifying information, including name, occupation and original cause of death. To evaluate the deaths, medical examiners were provided with a rating sheet for each case which consisted of a ten-point interval scale ranging from one ("not at all a suicide") to ten ("definitely a suicide"). A mean score of six or greater for the three medical examiners was considered grounds for reclassification to suicide. Medical examiners were also asked for a written statement concerning the basis and reasons for their ranking. Deaths originally classified as accidents or undetermined, but subsequently judged by the medical examiner panel as suicides, were reclassified as suicides. Medical examiners reclassified four police officers and one municipal worker death classification to suicide. There were no suicides originally classified as suicides that were changed to non-suicides. Table 5 lists reclassified deaths.

Table 4

SUMMARY OF MEDICAL EXAMINER PANEL RECLASSIFICATION TO SUICIDE

Case #	Original Death Classification	Description	Occupation Performed	Autopsy (1–10 Scale)	ME Mean Suicide Ratings
1	Undetermined	Gunshot wound to head	Police	Yes	9.5
2	Undetermined	Gunshot wound to head	Police	Yes	8.0
3	Undetermined	Gunshot wound to head	Police	Yes	9.0
4	Undetermined	Gunshot wound to head	Police	No	10.0
5	Accident	Drowning	Municipal	No	9.5

NOTE: Medical Examiner Interrater reliability = .976
SOURCE: Violanti et al. (in press). *Journal of Suicide and Life-Threatening Behavior.*

The validity of suicide rates may be estimated statistically in terms of "sensitivity"—the degree to which they correctly identify true suicides (O'Carroll, 1989). Thus, after death classifications were re-evaluated by the panel of medical examiners, police and municipal worker suicide rates were compared for sensitivity.

Results in Table 6 indicated that twenty (83.3%) police suicides originally classified as suicides remained suicides after the medical examiner panel's review. For municipal workers, twelve (92.3%) suicides originally classified as suicides remained suicides after panel review. None of the suicides originally classified as suicides were changed to non-suicides. What this means is that approximately 17 percent of police suicides, as opposed to 8 percent of suicides in other occupations, are being misclassified. As an example, for every 100 police suicides officially reported there may actually be 117 suicides.

Police Suicide

Table 5
SENSITIVITY VALUES OF SUICIDE RATES AMONG POLICE AND MUNICIPAL WORKERS

Official Death Classification	Adjusted Death Classification (ME Panel Evaluation) Standard		
Police Officers	Suicide	Not Suicide	Total
Suicide	20	0	20
Not Suicide	5	25	30
Total	25	25	50
Municipal Workers			
Suicide	12	0	12
Not Suicide	1	76	77
Total	13	76	89
	Police	Municipal Workers	
Sensitivity	83.3%	92.3%	

NOTE: N = 138
SOURCE: Violanti et al. (in press). *Journal of Suicide and Life-Threatening Behavior.*

Chapter 4

PRECIPITANTS OF SUICIDE: EXPOSURE TO STRESS AND TRAUMATIC INCIDENTS

STRESS IN POLICE WORK

M uch has been written about stress in the police occupation. Hans Selye (1978), a pioneer researcher in the field of stress, first noted that police work was likely one of the most stressful occupations in the world. Although some researchers argue that police work has not been adequately compared to other occupations (Terry, 1981, 1983; Swanson & Territo, 1983; Gaines, Southerland & Angell, 1991), they still agree that officers experience stress-related problems in their work.

Factors related to stress in police work have been categorized in various ways, including organizational practices and characteristics, the criminal justice system, the public, and the inherent nature of police work (Territo & Vetter, 1981; Stratton, 1978; Reese, 1986). Of these categories, two appear to emerge as most bothersome to officers: organizational practices and the inherent nature of police work itself (Spielberger, Westberry, Grier & Greenfield, 1981; Martelli, Waters & Martelli, 1989).

Similar to other occupations, organizational and interdepartmental practices are a continuous source of distress in police work. Among the factors which cause distress are authoritarian structure, lack of participation in decisions affecting daily work tasks, lack of administrative support, a punishment-centered philosophy, and unfair discipline (Kroes, 1986; Ellison & Genz, 1983; Reiser, 1974; Violanti, 1978; Kelling & Pate, 1975). Officers often view the organization as non-supportive and unresponsive to their needs (Perrier & Toner, 1984). Another facet involves administrative functions, including the requirement to ask "permission" for simple things like office supplies or taking a personal leave day. The promotion process is often perceived as lacking in integrity, and external influences from politicians can filter down to the lowest subordinate (Aron, 1992).

Stressors reported as inherent in police work are danger, shift work, public apathy, boredom, a sense of uselessness, and dealing with misery and death (Kroes, 1986; Territo & Vetter, 1981; Symonds, 1970; Graf, 1986, Spielberger et al., 1981). Danger may take several forms, including known danger during undercover work and unexpected danger such as stopping a vehicle or entering a building (Aron, 1992). Rotating shifts often lead to inadequate sleep for officers, which lowers physiological resistance to stress (Violanti, 1986). Boredom in the routine of everyday police functions may lead to a sense of uselessness and frustration (Kroes, 1986). Exposure to human suffering and death may also result in an extreme negative view of life and occupation.

Stress and Suicide

Inconsistencies in availability and accuracy of police suicide data, differences in individual vulnerability, and differential exposure to stress across police departments make researching stress and suicide difficult. Kappeler, Blumberg, and Potter (1993) argue that the connection between police stress and suicide is a "myth" which perpetuates public perception of "battered and blue crime-fighters." Other researchers have attributed police suicide more to the fact that: (1) the police occupation is male dominated and statistically males commit suicide more often than females, and (2) officers have a readily available, lethal method with which to commit suicide (Alpert & Dunham, 1988). Still others attribute police suicide to the consequences of uncovering corruption in departments. Friedman (1968), for example, cited the fact that many of the suicides in the New York City Police Department in the 1930s was possibly related to the Tammany Hall corruption scandal. Recent police suicides in New York City could possibly be related to a drug ring investigation. Several of the twelve officers who committed suicide in 1994 were part of that investigation.

Despite the interaction of other precipitants, it is still possible that stress, and/or the inability to adequately cope with stress, may play an integral part in police suicide. McCafferty, McCafferty, and McCafferty (1992) comment on suicide and stress:

> Stress is not always harmful; it is the individual's reaction to stress that determines whether they will adapt or become maladaptive. One individual's intolerable stress can be another's challenge. It is the type and severity of stress this particular individual faces, with his psychologic makeup and coping mechanisms, neurobiologic substrate, and social support systems . . . that deter-

mine the ultimate outcome.... For those individuals who feel powerless or hopeless, suicide may be a means of taking control over their helplessness.

It is also possible that chronic exposure to stress may lead to symptomatic emotional numbing in officers that may make death easier to accept as a coping solution (DSM–IV, American Psychiatric Association, 1994). McCafferty et al. (1992) comment:

> It would be impossible to adequately prepare an individual in the police academy for the stress encountered on the street. There is almost continual psychologic pressure in police work because the officer must be prepared even if nothing is happening. The constant reminder of the badge and the weight of the pistol on the hip serves notice that at any moment a police officer may be called upon to use deadly force to cope with a sudden life-threatening situation. There is constant exposure to hostility, anger, aggression, depression, and tragedy in the various events and confrontations that occur daily in a police officer's life. The constant exposure to these sorts of stress requires the officer to use all of his adaptive mechanisms to cope.... The ultimate result in some individuals is despair, alienation, isolation, a sense of futility, hopelessness, and finally suicide.

Stress and the Police Family

The police officer is not the only one affected by job stress. At home, officers tend to shut down emotions towards the family, leading to a process of detachment and the seeking of outside relationships (Hageman, 1978). Stratton (1978) found that officers experienced a high divorce rate, although this has been disputed by other researchers (Niederhoffer & Niederhoffer, 1986). Friedman (1968) and Danto (1978) concluded that marital troubles were the precipitating factor in the majority of suicide cases they studied. For the officer who feels powerless and overwhelmed by stress, the spouse may be the final resource to turn to for emotional protection and feelings of self-worth. However, officers have difficulty admitting feelings of helplessness and depression to themselves, much less to a spouse (Bonafacio, 1991).

Danieli (personal communication, 1994) suggests that exposure to stress and trauma may lead to trans-generational transmission of suicide to members of the police family. Horn (personal communication, 1994) described a case of an FBI agent who killed himself in his office to "get even with a supervisor," but didn't realize the lifelong pain he inflicted on his family and what a lesson he taught his children about how to deal with problems. Danieli commented on a case of a son of an officer who committed suicide four years after his father by firing the bullet into his head exactly at the same point that his father did. Kamerman (1993), in his study of New York City police suicides, provided an example of the effects of suicide on police family members:

> A son became an alcoholic a year or so after finding out that his father, a police officer, had committed suicide. His older brother, who was four years old when his father died, also found out at sixteen that his father had killed himself. The older son died in a boating accident in his mid-forties. . . . He once told his brother that "the best way for him to go (die) would be to drown," and that's exactly how he died. (p. 352)

Future research might consider an analysis of suicides within police families. The present author has knowledge of at least four suicides of police officers' sons, all of whom shot themselves with their father's gun.

TRAUMATIC STRESS IN POLICE WORK

Of the factors associated with stress in policing, incidents outside the range of normal occurrences appear to adversely affect officers. Such events are termed "critical incidents" and may include shootings, witnessing death and mutilation, attending to disasters, and dealing with abused or maltreated children.

Critical incidents are often rated by police officers as highly stressful. The present author found that "killing someone in the line of duty," "death of a fellow officer," and "physical attack" were ranked as the top three stressors by police officers (Violanti & Aron, 1994). Often associated with critical incidents is a prolonged reaction classified as posttraumatic stress disorder (PTSD). PTSD occurs when the officer has been exposed to a traumatic event and persistently re-experiences and avoids stimuli associated with that event. The officer may also experience symptoms of increased physiological arousal because of the trauma. These criteria can persist for several months and even years in some cases (American Psychiatric Association, DSM–IV, 1994, p. 428).

Nielson (1986) points out that the impact of a critical incident may depend on several factors. First, the more sudden and unexpected the occurrence, the more likely it will adversely affect the officer. For example, police officers involved in "ambush" type shootings are more susceptible to trauma than those who are part of a prepared assault or have previous information on a possible traumatic incident.

Secondly, the incident may have a negative psychological impact when it results in a serious threat to the officer's existence and well-being. An officer's involvement in a shooting, for example, is generally followed by a departmental investigation, grand jury testimony, media exposure, and possible physical injury. These may lead to a perceived threat of losing one's job or being indicted for a wrongful shooting. Officers who are themselves shot may experience physically disabling effects which are threatening to their quality of life.

Third, the incident may include an element of loss for the officer. It may be a personal loss, such as use of a limb, or it may be the loss of a patrol partner who was killed. The severity of such loss may be directly related to the intensity of trauma. Lastly, the impact of trauma on police officers may depend strongly on the degree of disruption of personal and social values. An officer who has killed someone, for example, may be affected by the moral issue of taking a human life.

Officers have reported prolonged symptoms in response to work-related incidents months after the event occurred. A study conducted by Mantell (1988) in San Diego found that approximately 50 percent of the officers involved in the McDonald's restaurant killings in that city had symptoms of PTSD. Mantell commented about the scene of that crime:

> The officers, 200 or more, at the scene of the San Ysidro McDonald's massacre, were able to mask their emotions by channeling their feelings into their jobs. They were able to divorce themselves from the reality of dead children lying in blood—with Ronald McDonald standing over them, smiling. But, some could not. "You know, doc, I'm sick to my stomach seeing those kids in there. I can't stop seeing my own two kids—you know they are the same age practically and I swear when I kissed them good-bye this morning, my oldest was wearing the same shirt on that blood-drenched kid over there" (p. 358).

Martin, McKean and Veltkamp (1986) found that 26 percent of their police sample experienced PTSD symptoms one month or longer following exposure to traumatic work events. Stratton, Parker, and Snibbe (1984) found that approximately 30 percent of their police sample reported that a shooting incident affected them greatly. Officers exposed to such events reported higher percentages of PTSD symptoms than those not exposed. The greatest percentage of symptoms were reported by officers involved in shootings and those whose families were threatened (Martin et al., p. 100). Loo (1986) found that officers experienced the most stress reactions within three days after the incident. In his data, the majority of officers reported preoccupation with the traumatic incident (39%) and anger (25%). Other reported symptoms of PTSD were sleep disturbances, flashbacks, guilt feelings, wishing it didn't happen, and depression. Many of the officers continued to report increased anger and lowered work interest after one month post-incident. The course of recovery varied for officers, but the average time of "feeling normal" was 20 weeks after the critical work incident.

Traumatic Stress: Relationships to Police Suicide

Suicide may be an attempt of police officers to restore feelings of strength, courage, and mastery over the environment after exposure to a traumatic incident. Such deaths may be prompted by a perceived loss of coping abilities and a feeling of vulnerability not experienced prior to the incident (Allen, 1986; Bonafacio, 1991; Heiman, 1977; McCafferty et al., 1992; Violanti, 1990).

Early studies hint at the association between traumatic incidents and police suicide. Danto (1978), for example, found that many officers in the Detroit police who committed suicide were exposed to some type of job-related trauma. Eleven of the 12 officers had been injured on the job due to confrontations with citizens, and all had been involved in a traffic accident during their careers. Two of the officers had received wound medals for on-duty shootings. Danto's investigation also revealed that many of these officers expressed guilt over shooting incidents. A study of the Royal Canadian Mounted Police by Loo (1986) found that 15 percent of officers who committed suicide were recently exposed to a traumatic work incident involving either the suicide of a close friend or a serious motor vehicle accident.

Shattered Illusions of Invulnerability

A suspected precursor of suicide concerns the negative impact that trauma has on the police image of invulnerability. The strong socialization which occurs in police training and experience instills in officers a sense of superhuman emotional and survival strength to deal with adversity. From the very first day in the police academy, recruit officers are told that they are someone unique, far different from the average citizen and certainly beyond psychological harm.

This pervasive illusion of invulnerability seems to be prevalent among new officers and is similar to Burger and Burns' (1988) concept of "unique invulnerability" found in adolescents. One component of this concept is the "personal fable" (Elkind, 1967), a feeling that one is unique and has feelings and experiences unlike any other person. This feeling is reinforced by a strong belief in one's indestructibility (Greening & Dollinger, 1992). Because of this perception of invulnerability, officers learn to shut off their feelings towards various situations at work. Seeing a dead child or a mangled accident victim must, in the minds of officers, become part of the job and nothing more.

The officer whose traumatic experiences penetrate this psychological shield may feel vulnerable for a long period afterward and never again regain the sense of being uniquely protected from harm. Greening and Dollinger (1992), in their study on disaster victims, found that effects of shattered notions of invulnerability lasted for as long as seven years. Even time-limited shattered notions of invulnerability can leave a permanent effect on the officers when they face similar future events. Rangell (1967) suggests that trauma deals a strong blow to the ego, causing a feeling of lack of control, vulnerability, and of not being able to cope with future occurrences.

Trauma and Suicide

While being emotionally impenetrable is considered necessary by officers in police work, it may also increase the likelihood of suicide when the "armor" is suddenly shattered by stress and traumatic events. Feelings of vulnerability may affect coping ability, but it is not yet understood precisely what those effects are. It is known that people experience differential vulnerability, as some cope satisfactorily with trauma while others do not (Fowlie & Aveline, 1985; Frye & Stockton, 1982; Foy, Sipprelle, Rueger & Carroll, 1984; Kessler, 1979). Police officers expect not to feel vulnerable; when they do, it brings feelings of shame, fear, and a heightened sense of danger.

Suicide may become an option as the officer attempts to adapt to shattered perceptions of invulnerability. The denial of mortality becomes progressively more difficult for officers, and the effect of confrontation with hostile people takes its toll. To overcome emotional numbing associated with trauma, the officer seeks increased stimulation. The result may be outrageous behavior, involvement in casual sexual affairs, impulsiveness, and aggressive actions. Suicide may be the result from the lack of an outlet for these behaviors and a final coping strategy for unendurable psychological pain (McCafferty et al., 1992).

Civilian Combat: Trauma Stress and Suicide

Military combat and police work often share similar conditions and outcomes (Williams, 1987; Violanti, in press). Both soldiers and police officers experience events in their work which significantly increase psychological trauma. Williams (1987) describes police officers as being involved in "peacetime combat":

> For cops, the war never ends.... They are out there 24 hours a day, 7 days a week to protect and serve, to fight the criminal—our peacetime enemy. The police officer is expected to be combat-ready at all times while remaining normal and socially adaptive when away from the job. The psychological toll for many is great, unexpected, and not well understood. (p. 267)

Violanti (in press) stated that police officers experience similar conditions to Vietnam veterans: (1) an unknown enemy, (2) a continual sense of insecurity, (3) lack of public support, (3) witnessing abusive violence, and (4) depersonalization (Laufer, Gallops & Frey-Wouters, 1984). Even some of the aftereffects are similar among Vietnam veterans and police officers:

Suicide. The suicide rate for Vietnam veterans is 33 percent higher than the general population.

Alcohol Abuse. Alcohol-related problems among Vietnam veterans has doubled within the past seven years. Among police, an estimated 15–25 percent are believed to be dependent on alcohol. This is evidenced by the significantly high death rate for cirrhosis of the liver among police officers (Violanti & Vena, 1986; Vena & Violanti, 1986).

Family life. Thirty-eight percent of Vietnam veterans were divorced within six months after their return home. They found it difficult to establish interpersonal relationships, likely due to a hardening of emotions. Police divorce rates indicate a similar disruption in family life. A large percentage of police marriages end in divorce (estimates from 60%–75%) (Stratton, 1984).

Integration into Society. Vietnam soldiers returned home with little chance to adjust. In essence, they were flung from the ricelands of Vietnam into the streets of America. As one soldier said: "One day, I was killing Viet Cong, the next I was having a beer at a local bar back home" (Violanti, 1983). The police officer experiences a similar uneasy transition everyday. He/she must go from the stressful, sometimes violent nature of police work to the normalcy of community and family life.

The exposure of police officers to the trauma of combat-like situations may be a possible precipitant to suicide. An early study by Simon (1950) found that over half of World War Two veterans who committed suicide were in combat. He suggested that combat or combat-like conditions may evoke aggressive impulses which eventually turn on the self. Pokorny (1967) found that younger male World War Two veterans were more likely to commit suicide than males in the general population, and that the presence of psychiatric illness among those veterans led to a nine-fold increase in suicide.

Recent studies concerning the relationship of combat and suicide focus on Vietnam veterans. Higher rates of post-service suicide have been reported among Vietnam veterans (Hearst, Newman & Tully, 1986). One the largest studies completed on the relationship of suicide and combat conditions was done by the Centers for Disease Control (1987). Examination of external cause of death among combat veterans showed that they had significantly higher mortality from motor vehicle accidents, homicide, and suicide. The excess was most pronounced during the first five years after discharge. For suicide, the rate among combat veterans was 72 percent higher than the general population. Farberow, Kang, and Bullman (1990) examined the potential risk factors for suicide among veterans involved in combat and veterans who died from civilian motor vehicle accidents. Their findings indicated that 72 percent of the combat veterans who committed suicide were depressed, compared to 10 percent of the accident group. Veteran suicides also seemed to have experienced more posttraumatic stress symptoms than non-veterans.

Hendin and Haas (1991) attempted to identify predictors of suicide among combat veterans with posttraumatic stress disorder. Of 100 veterans, 19 had committed suicide and 15 had attempted suicide. The authors found that guilt played a major role in precipitating suicide; veterans felt guilty about actions they took that led to death while in combat and about surviving when others had died. Hendin and Haas concluded that the affective state of the person at the time of combat actions was an important motivation for suicide:

> The need for punishment based on combat guilt or survivor guilt was not the only motivation for suicide. For some veterans, the sense of having been transformed by combat experiences into a "murderer," in danger of again losing control of feelings of aggression and rage, was a significant motivating factor. (Hendin & Haas, p. 590)

An interesting part of many of these studies concerns the types of critical incidents that veterans who committed suicide experienced in

Vietnam. Many of these incidents were *similar in nature to those reported by police officers.* For example, Farberow et al. (1990) found the following distributions of critical experiences among their veteran suicide sample: 64 percent saw death, 54 percent were fired upon, 27 percent were responsible for the death of an enemy soldier, 18 percent were wounded, 14 percent witnessed atrocities, and 36 percent reported an extremely stressful combat experience.

COPING WITH STRESS AND TRAUMA

Police officers often comment that they feel helpless and ineffective in dealing with the vast amount of crime in this country. Peck (1984) stated that suicidal behavior can be attributed in part to stress-related reactions to the person's perceived inability to act upon social conditions and events causing traumatic stress. Suicide may be a result of the officer's inability to accept failure and to cope with stress or trauma:

> Motivations to suicide include a breakdown of intimate relationships and the inability to accept situational arrangements dictated by others. One obstacle to social and psychological well-being among committees was the recognition that they were powerless to act as an effective force on behalf of their own best interests. Obstacles to personal well-being appear to contribute to the decision to suicide; the taking of one's own life may be the final effort to control an outcome. (Peck, 1984, p. 12)

Suicide is frequently thought of as an ultimate coping response to an intolerable condition. Suicidal police officers may, in effect, exhaust all available coping strategies to deal with the stress of their jobs. The result may be what Shneidman (1985) termed "constriction" of thought, a condition of limited response to a situation. Officers in a state of constriction can only perceive two alternatives: remove the intolerable condition or die. Since it is unlikely that the conditions of exposure in police work will change, the suicidal officer may choose death.

The Police and Coping

Most people can find alternative ways to cope with situations other than suicide. Police officers as a group, however, tend not to cope well with psychological distress and often turn to maladaptive coping strategies (Violanti, 1993a). Coping skills may be defined as behavioral reactions to distress, and two primary categories of coping strategies have been identified: emotion and problem-focused strategies (Lazarus, 1981). Hovanitz (1986) reported that emotion-focused strategies are generally less successful than problem-focused strategies. In a recent study, Lennings (1994) found that police officers tend to use problem-solving coping strategies less than non-police persons (Toch & Grant, 1991). This was seen as unusual, since police generally perceive themselves as problem solvers. Although police may use some problem-solving techniques, it appears such techniques are primarily defensive in nature and may lead to inaccurate appraisals of a stressful situation (Fridell & Binder, 1992).

Violanti (1993b) found that police officers primarily turned to two types of coping when confronted with stress: "escape avoidance" and "distancing." Escape avoidance involves avoidance of people and the use of alcohol or drugs, and distancing involves emotional escape from the situation. Distancing is distinctly different from escape coping; one can distance oneself psychologically from a situation but may not be able to escape or avoid the consequences of that same situation. Highly distressed officers likely use escape avoidance and distancing to deal with the lack of personal control in their work. Distancing may lead to depersonalization, which has been noted as a prominent feature of individual police behavior and culture (Pogrebin & Poole, 1991; Violanti, 1983, 1993c). For the police, these strategies may be maladaptive, as evidenced by increasing alienation, stress, and reliance on alcohol to manage the stress (Violanti, Marshall & Howe, 1983).

The police training environment may contribute to the inefficacy of police coping abilities. Violanti (1993a) suggested that the use of distancing, self-controlling, accepting personal responsibility, and escape-avoidance were employed significantly more by recruits under high distress. Escape-avoidance and distancing have an especially strong maladaptive potential. It is also possible that the training academy experience may increase the use of such strategies. If counterbalancing socialization does not occur after the recruit leaves the academy, the possibility exists that such strategies might well carry over into the work environment. A lower stress training environment may allow for a wider choice of behavior conducive to proper coping and adjustment to police work.

The research suggests that police get into trouble at least some of the time because of perceived appraisal strategies. Either they are unaware of people's feelings and situations, unaware of their own anxiety in a situation, or have made a judgment based upon an inflexible plan that is rigidly followed (Fridell & Binder, 1992; Pogrebin & Poole, 1991; Stotland, 1991). Even maladaptive coping techniques, however, may break down over time in officers (Selye, 1978; Somodevilla, 1986). Given evidence of the lack of viable coping alternatives in police work and the primary socialization of officers into potentially maladaptive coping strategies, it is possible that suicide may become a final coping alternative. Perhaps training officers in problem-solving, emotion-focusing, and decision-making strategies may provide them with coping alternatives to suicide (Bayley, 1986).

Chapter 5

OTHER FACTORS IN POLICE SUICIDE: GUNS, ALCOHOL, AND RETIREMENT

SUICIDE AND FIREARMS

Trends in the general population indicate that the presence of firearms increases the probability of suicide. In the United States, firearms are the most common method of suicide, and the volume of firearm deaths for suicide was higher than homicide or accidents in 1990 (Centers for Disease Control, 1985; Shaffer & Fisher, 1981). Deaths from suicide and homicide combined were the third leading cause of years of potential life lost before age 65 in 1991 in the United States. Firearms were used in 60.1 percent of all suicides. From 1980 to 1991, approximately *one million years of potential life* were lost due to firearm-related deaths, which represents an increase of 13.6 percent over previous decades, in comparison with a 25.2 percent decrease in heart disease and a 1.1 percent increase in cancer. Firearm-related suicides increased from 45.6 percent to 48.3 percent during this same time period, exceeding firearm use in homicides. If present trends continue, firearm-related injuries will become the leading cause of injury-related mortality in the United States (NIH Morbidity and Mortality Weekly Report, October, 1994).

Police Suicide and Availability of Firearms

The firearm is more than just a work tool to police officers; it is a symbol of their authority, identity as guardians of law, and mastery over the environment. The value of the police firearm becomes obvious when it is taken away. An officer comments:

> I was involved in a shooting, and right away internal affairs came in and took away my gun. They said they needed it for evidence purposes and it was to be sent to the lab for analysis. There I was, walking around the scene without a gun in my holster. What a horrible feeling. The next day, the captain tells me that I have to work inside at headquarters for a couple of weeks while the investigation on the shooting is completed. I was in the "rubber gun" squad, a

desk-jockey. It was demeaning and I was embarrassed in front of my police friends. I felt powerless.

The police firearm becomes the officer's physical and psychological shield at work. As long as the gun is there, visible to all, it puts the officer "one-up" on the rest of society. The symbolic value of the police firearm may make it quite fitting for the ultimate act of coping with adversity: suicide. The author's present research indicates that police officers have a *6.4-fold risk* of committing suicide with a gun than do other occupations (Violanti & Vena, research in progress).

The basic question is whether the number of police suicides is higher than the number that would have occurred if guns were not available. The answer to this question is related to the ready availability of firearms. Accessibility of firearms is likely an important precipitant in police suicide, since officers have immediate access both on and off-duty. Many police agencies encourage officers to carry a loaded service firearm off-duty in case of immediate emergency needs. Reported police suicides increase in such agencies (Ivanoff, 1994).

The police have a higher rate of firearm suicide than other groups who work with firearms. The military is one example, where firearms are available *but not as immediately accessible* as they are to police officers. Generally, military personnel are required to turn in weapons at base storage facilities and do not carry them to residences or barracks. Although the most common method of suicide in the military is by firearm, approximately 59 percent of military personnel compared to 95 percent of police officers use a firearm (Moldeven, 1994; Violanti & Vena, research in progress). The police also have a higher rate of suicide by firearms than persons who possess guns in their home. Kellerman et al. (1992) studied suicides over a 32-month period found that 58% of all suicides were committed with a firearm.

The present author's research found that not only did officers use their firearms 95 percent of the time to commit suicide but also that they did it 90 percent of the time away from the work place. This was more than twice the rate of suicides away from the work place in the military, where 43 percent of firearm suicides were at the victim's residence (Moldeven, 1994). This finding adds credence to the idea that 24-hour accessibility to firearms may increase the risk of suicide in police officers.

Additional studies have commented on police use of firearms for suicide. Labovitz and Hagedorn (1971) and Nelson and Smith (1970) reported that high police suicide rates are a result of accessibility to firearms within the context of occupational exposure to death and injury; social strain, criminal justice inconsistencies; and a negative police image. Aussant (1984) found that firearms were used in 80 percent of police suicides in Quebec. Danto (1978) found firearms and carbon monoxide poisoning to be the most common forms of suicide in Detroit police officers. Friedman (1968) found that the suicide rate among *armed* officers in New York City was twice that of the general population, while *unarmed* London police officers had a rate similar to the general population. Kellerman et al. (1992) found that persons who carry loaded firearms were more likely to use them in a suicide; few victims acquired their guns within hours or days of the suicide, and the vast majority had guns at home.

Thus, decisions by police officers to commit suicide might never be acted on if substantial efforts were necessary to arrange for suicide method (O'Carroll, Rosenberg, & Mercy, 1991). Because suicide with a firearm is often immediately lethal, officers have the opportunity to commit suicide impulsively with little or no time to consider the action. Accessibility to firearms may also limit any pre-attempt opportunity for intervention by others.

Given that the majority of police officers commit suicide with a fire-arm and generally do so off-duty away from the work place, it follows that some suicides may be prevented by limiting access to firearms. The practice of requiring police to carry firearms off-duty may be an important target for police organizational policy change. Limiting access may work because suicide impulses are often quite transitory. Persons whose preferred method of suicide is unavailable often *do not* resort to other means, and suicides are usually performed by means already available to the person rather than by means to be obtained specifically to commit suicide. Browning (1974) found that only about 10 percent of firearm suicides were performed by firearms purchased specifically for that purpose; the other 90 percent were committed by firearms already available to the person.

ALCOHOL AND SUICIDE

Recent community studies indicate that alcohol dependency contributes to approximately 25 percent of all suicides a year in the United States (Rich, Young & Fowler, 1986; Arato, Demeter, Rihmer & Somogyi,

1988; Asgard, 1990; Murphy, 1992). Murphy (1992) found that continued drinking is an important risk factor for suicide.

Alcohol use has been found to be a factor in suicide, and police use of alcohol may be precipitated by stress. Violanti et al. (1983) found a significant positive relationship between alcohol use and stress among police officers. Beutler, Nussbaum, and Meredith (1988) found increased time in police service to be associated with maladaptive responses by officers. Even early in the police career, officers tended to respond negatively to the demands of police work by addictive alcohol use. Romanov et al. (1994), in a study of over 21,000 adults, found increased alcohol use to lead to a 2.5-fold risk of suicide.

Precise figures for alcoholism among police officers are not available, but reports indicate that more than 25 percent of officers have serious problems related to alcohol abuse (Kroes, 1986). In the Chicago police suicide study, alcoholism was documented in 12 of 20 suicides. In addition, these twelve officers had extensive medical records, six (30%) had average records, and two had limited medical records. The majority of medical complaints were stomach flu, nervous problems, high blood pressure, heart trouble, back trouble, kidney disease, bursitis, and alcoholism. Discipline records revealed that 7 of the 20 had serious discipline problems, seven had normal discipline records, and six had no discipline problems (Cronin, 1982).

Alcohol is an important problem in police work and may lead to other work problems such as high absenteeism, intoxication on duty, complaints by supervisors and citizens of misconduct on duty, traffic accidents, and an overall decrease in work performance (Violanti et al., 1983, McCafferty et al., 1992). Skolnick (1972) commented that police officers are by no means abstainers and that they usually drink together to avoid public criticism. Unkovic and Brown (1976) found that 8 percent of their category labeled "heavy drinkers" were police officers. Van Raalte (1979) reports that 67 percent of his police sample admitted drinking on duty. He also cites several instances of intoxicated off-duty officers injuring others with a firearm. Hitz (1973) found police mortality ratios for alcohol-related cirrhosis of the liver to be significantly higher than the general population. Wagner and Brzeczek (1983) documented alcohol abuse in 60 percent of suicides in the Chicago Police Department. Violanti et al. (1983) reported a statistically significant relationship between stress and alcohol use among police officers.

Alcohol use among police may be underestimated. Many officers, fearing departmental discipline, are unwilling to officially report their dependence. Police organizations appear ambivalent towards drinking problems, placing blame on the individual officer and not the police occupational structure. Other departments may "hide" problem drinkers in positions where they will not adversely affect police operations (Kroes, 1986).

Besides alcohol, drug use may be an increasing problem in policing. McCafferty et al. (1992) commented that drug abuse is becoming a problem for police departments as more officers begin to use drugs or are hired with the habit already established. A police officer with a weapon who is abusing drugs is a risk to himself, his family, his fellow police officers, and the public.

RETIREMENT

The present author conducted a study of suicide committed by retired police officers in Buffalo, New York between 1950 and 1990. Suicide rates for retired officers were similar to other occupations but were significantly higher in officers just *prior* to retirement. Apparently, this time period was psychologically difficult for these officers and psychological mal-adaption resulted. Gaska (1980) conducted a study of suicide among 4,000 retired officers of the Detroit Police Department from 1944–1978 and found an increased risk of suicide. Suicide rates for these officers was 334.7/100,000 compared to 11.1/100,000 for the general population. If the officer was retired due to a disability, the rate increased to 2,616/100,000. Gaska added that two-thirds of the suicides in his study were originally classified as accidental or natural deaths in order to protect the department and family members. With these findings in mind, it is important to discuss some possible reasons for suicide among pre-retired and retired officers.

Factors in Police Retirement

For the police officer, retirement can be a difficult time. In police work, a strong camaraderie develops among officers. They liken themselves to the military, where survival depends on individuals working as a close team. When an officer leaves the ranks, the loss is experienced by all concerned. Police officers have a love-hate relationship with their jobs; they find it difficult to stay beyond 20 years and even more difficult to leave.

Retired officers are generally not prepared to become "civilians." Involved is a loss of police power and a feeling that one is no longer part of the police family. To leave this interpersonal web of protection is not easy for police officers. It is as if someone had removed an integral part of their personality. An officer comments:

> It's like I belonged to a big club. I made my mark, I was one of the guys, I did my job. Everyone in the station respects you and you get along good with the sergeants and lieutenants. Suddenly all of that is gone and you are on the outside looking in. I felt so different. I called the guys almost everyday to see if they still related to me the same way. I visited the station, wondering what was going on and wanting to be part of the action. I played golf with the guys, went to all the parties. Somehow, it wasn't the same. I wasn't one of them anymore. It's hard to explain. I retired, but I couldn't let go of this strong attachment. (Violanti, 1992)

Finding relationships which substitute for the police subculture can be difficult for retired officers. There is a marked contrast between the roles of being a police officer and a civilian. The structure of police work is very similar to that of the military. As McNeill, Lecca, and Wright (1983) pointed out, each individual's role in a military-like structure is predetermined through tradition and written regulation. Many police officers feel very insecure without the structure they have been used to for 20–25 years. They do not know what type of role to occupy and may spend considerable time seeking out activities in which to structure their retired lives.

Retirement can have serious psychological consequences for police officers. It is a time when some officers experience alcoholism and possibly suicide. An example was an officer who had one dream: to retire after 20 years, collect his pension, and sell used cars. He did just that, and for a year or so, things were great. Then he began to drink incessantly and eventually became an alcoholic. He experienced a period of depression and talked of nothing but his time as a police officer. At one point, he made the decision to commit suicide but changed his mind at the very last second. Since his episode of depression, he has readjusted somewhat but still must deal with periods of emotional problems.

As officers approach twenty years of service, many conflicting attitudes occur. Thoughts turn to "what do I do now?" Often much of the rhetoric of the past few years about getting out seem to be "words spoken too soon." Many officers face a conflict in emotions as this time; they want to leave, but they experience the fear of being out in civilian life. Many middle-aged police officers appear to be in a retirement identity crisis. On the one hand, they develop a cynical attitude about police work, complain incessantly about administration, dislike their work, and feel trapped in their jobs because of pensions. On the other hand, they struggle with separation from the close identity they developed towards police work (Violanti, 1992).

The "waiters" retire in bitter haste, proclaiming that they can't wait to leave the job. Previous experience shows that these officers generally do not fare out well after retirement. Their bitterness and cynicism seem to carry over into their retirement and they develop a very negative view of life. These officers have the highest potential for suicide. Those who decide not to retire may also experience personal and psychological difficulties if things do not change for them. Fortunately for some, things do improve and they regain a positive outlook towards police work. They are the lucky ones who cope successfully with the retirement crisis.

Certain factors make police retirement difficult. First is advancing age. Officers begin to realize that if they want employment opportunities after their police careers they had better take action. If officers retire at 40–45 years of age, they likely have an increased probability of getting another job. If they stay past the age of fifty, opportunities for work decrease. Second are barriers which constrain the decision to retire. Examples are financial obligations, mortgages, or college tuition for children. Third, changing circumstances on the job may increase the complexity of the retirement decision. For example, the officer may get promoted or be assigned a favorable position with enhanced working conditions. Others may want to leave because they do not get promoted and experience feelings of lowered self-esteem.

A common theme in these examples is blockage. Blockage from multiple sources in the police environment can be a source of extreme frustration and stress when an officer is faced with such an important decision as retirement. These are potential situations for suicide.

Chapter 6

THEORETICAL FOUNDATIONS
OF POLICE SUICIDE

Throughout this book, we have mentioned many ideas and concepts about suicide among police officers. Despite this myriad of research, there are few theoretical models of police suicide. In this chapter, we will review some important theoretical models, which will serve as a prelude to our own theoretical framework in Chapter 7.

GENERAL THEORY

Police suicide has been associated with availability and expertise of firearms, continuous duty exposure to death and injury, shift work, social strain, criminal justice inconsistencies, and a negative police image (Labovitz & Hagedorn, 1971; Nelson & Smith, 1970). Likely the first major study conducted was that of Friedman (1968), who conducted a study of 93 police suicides in New York City from 1930–1940. Friedman found the rate for officers to be 6.5 times that of the general population. He attributed such high rates to two factors: aggression turned inward and the circumstances of the political climate. Friedman's "aggression" model was based on a psychoanalytic concept of pent-up hostility:

No one kills himself who has never wanted to kill another . . . or at least wished the death of another . . . the unconscious court condemns the self . . . eye for an eye, tooth for a tooth . . . it declares itself guilty of the death wish and condemns itself to death.

Shneidman (1970) provided a similar concept of suicide as being "murder in the 180th degree." Shneidman based his idea on Freud's formulation of suicide as hostility directed towards the introjected "love object," and Menninger's components of suicide as "the wish to kill, the wish to be killed, and the wish to die" (Menninger, 1938). More recently, Romanov et al. (1994) found a 3.4-fold increased risk of suicide in persons with high hostility scores.

Heiman (1975) concluded that aggression alone did not account for high rates of police suicide. The exposure of officers to tragedy and human misery was also a motivating factor in police suicide. Heiman (1975) conducted a second study comparing New York City and London police suicides and found rates in New York to be twice that of the population, while London police rates were at par with the population. Heiman attributed high suicide rates in the United States to the availability of firearms and the negative public image of police. Lester (1993) later conducted a secondary analysis of Friedman's data and found that officers who committed suicide experienced depression (25%), paranoid ideation prior to the suicide (13%), problems at work (24%), were married (84%), were at a lower rank (84%), and had personal motives for suicide (65%). Alcohol abuse among these officers was significantly associated with depression, problems at work, and being at the lowest rank.

Danto (1978) conducted a study of twelve Detroit police suicides which occurred between 1968–1976. Two of the officers were over age 40, three in their early thirties, and seven in their late twenties. Most had served less than 10 years as a police officer. Six of the officers committed suicide at home and 66 percent used a firearm. Marital relationship problems appeared to be the most important precipitating factor in these suicides. Danto also commented on the impersonal nature of the police military structure and the lack of services for troubled officers. He advised the establishment of psychological counseling programs in police departments to provide ongoing assistance to officers.

Aussant (1984), in a study of Quebec police suicides, found that 80 percent of suicide victims used firearms, 50 percent had a history of psychiatric and/or medical problems, and many had a severe alcohol problem. Schwartz and Schwartz (1975) found that suicide rates were higher among older police officers and related to alcoholism, physical illness, or impending retirement. Nix (1986) commented that the police bureaucracy, with its military structure, overbearing regulations and negativism, was a primary catalyst in police suicides. Slater and Depue (1981) attributed police suicide to isolation of victim officers from the police culture. Violanti (1984) viewed police suicide as a response of officers to lack of control over work and personal lives.

Janik and Kravitz (1994) examined data from 134 police officers referred for fitness-for-duty evaluations and found that 55 percent admitted to previous suicide attempts. Results from this study indicated that an officer with marital problems was 4.8 times more likely to attempt suicide, 6.7 times more likely if they had been suspended for some wrongdoing, and 21.7 times more likely if both circumstances were present.

SELF-DESTRUCTIVE BEHAVIOR IN POLICE OFFICERS

Suicide as such may not always be readily identifiable. Certainly a final act of self-destruction is obvious, but some individuals may involve themselves in behaviors that Farberow (1980) defined as "indirect self-destructive behavior" (ISDB). ISDB occurs when the search for excitement and the degree of risk-taking exceeds considerations for safety or self-preservation. Many such individuals will provoke their difficulties which are often physically and socially destructive to themselves and persons close to them (Allen, 1986).

For police officers, the likelihood of developing indirect self-destructive behavior may be increased. The very nature of policing involves risk and has likely become part of their identities as police officers. Allen (1986), however, stated that identification with risk-taking can lead to psychological confusion for officers. If risk-taking is positive, the officer can grow by achieving the requirements of law enforcement. If risk-taking is negative, it can lead officers to disregard the possible effects of their actions and the fact that such actions may be suicidal.

Negative risk-taking is particularly dangerous because the need for excitement and danger can become compulsive or addictive. Therefore, behaviors which may be initially assessed as desirable in police work may in fact be early warning signs of impending self-destruction (Allen, 1986, p. 415).

Other behaviors among police may develop destructive behaviors over many years. For example, smoking, excessive alcohol use, or poor diet habits. Although no substantial evidence exists that such behavior is intentionally directed to self-destruction in police officers, some mortality studies show that officers tended to die at a greater ratio than the general population for heart disease, liver problems (alcohol), suicides, and homicides (Vena et al., 1986).

MAJOR THEORETICAL CONCEPTS OF POLICE SUICIDE

Freud (1935)

Perhaps the first attempt at a major theory of police suicide found its roots in the ideas of Sigmund Freud. To Freud, suicide was an expression of individual aggression and self-destruction. "Civilization," according to Freud, undermined the psychic health of members of the social group and threatened each of them with suicide (Litman, 1970). In many ways, Freud's idea of self-destruction led him to the concept of "death instinct," a destructive drive in each person whose final goal is annihilation. This dangerous drive is dealt with by individuals in various ways. Freud theorized that death wishes against oneself were in part rendered harmless by being diverted to the external world in the form of aggression. That is, if one holds back aggression, it can lead to "unhealthy" consequences such as suicide (Litman, 1970). Based on this, Freud recommended that there would be less suicide if society permitted its members to freely express aggression.

Freud's concept was likely the basis for future theories of police suicide. His ideas related easily to the police because they were strictly limited by the public and courts in any type of aggressive activity. Police officers were expected to use as little force as possible and to always be "pleasant" regardless of what others did or said to them. Pent-up anger and aggression could not be freely expressed under any circumstances.

Henry and Short (1954)

Henry and Short (1954) added a social dimension to Freud's psychodynamic model of aggression and suicide. These authors viewed aggressive behavior as stemming more from societal frustration rather than internal drives. As an act of aggression, suicide could not be differentiated from the source of the frustration which generates the aggression (society). In this sense, Henry and Short viewed suicide as aggression for which outward expression towards others is denied.

The primary difference between Freud and Henry and Short is that the latter viewed the *society* and not the individual as the precursor of aggressive suicide. However, similar to Freud, Henry and Short purported that frustration and the blockage of outward aggression may lead to suicide.

Friedman (1968)

Freud's concept of aggression and suicide was first applied to the police by Friedman (1968) in his analysis of 93 New York City police suicides:

> The law officer, even the most serene and conscientious, carries with him a complicated psychological structure: while defending the integrity of society and its citizens, he, like the soldier, must do it through extreme mobilization of inner powers of aggression which he always keeps available to work. In time, he gets disciplined ... and must submit instead of pushing others into submission; aggression becomes dammed up and turns upon the individual's self.... (Letter from Zilboorg to *New York Times,* 1938; in Friedman, 1968)

Police suicide cases studied by Friedman occurred during a tumultuous and corrupt period of time in the history of New York City (1934–1940). Police officers were often "socially licensed" to commit acts of aggression and corruption without penalty. When the government finally controlled corruption, many officers could not adjust:

> With the change, the hostile and aggressive police officer who formerly functioned with social license suddenly began to feel like a frustrated child. No one would support him, and everyone was against him or was unsympathetic. Some "took it out" on themselves by extreme alcoholism and illness; others, by aggressive and murderous acts—all eventually leading to so much pent-up hostility as to eventuate suicide. (Friedman, p. 428)

Friedman expected to find high rates of suicide among New York City officers due to the societal sanctioned use of power and aggression. He believed that such power led to a strong conflict in police officers:

> But, on the other hand, he (the officer) is also expected to refrain from killing and from other violent behavior. The aggressive and controlling drives, which are no doubt the primary motivations for choice of occupation, are often in collision with the command to refrain and repress, therefore causing tremendous conflict within.... (Friedman, p. 448)

Nelson and Smith (1970)

Nelson and Smith (1970) approached police suicide from a social perspective, applying Durkheim's (1966) explanation of social determinants as precipitants of human behavior. The police officer who committed suicide was seen as lacking integration into the society. Nelson and Smith hypothesized that officers are continuously disintegrated from society by the very nature of their jobs. The authors described police officers as not being particularly well liked for the work they do and as being isolated from society. They were seen as experiencing much more exposure to misery and death than average citizens. This coupled with strained family relationships and shift work isolated them even further. Nelson and Smith conclude:

> It appears that law enforcement officers often become alienated from others because of their particular work situations and social exclusion from those who want nothing to do with police and seem They bear almost a hatred for them. . . . If this be so, the presence of suicide potential in an occupational group of this orientation may be understandable. (p. 298)

Heiman (1975)

Heiman (1975) viewed social factors as covariates of aggression and police suicide. He thought it simplistic to think of police suicide as resulting from murderous aggression turned inward and argued that police are at a higher risk of suicide because of their relationship with society. Officers were viewed as being constantly exposed to human misery and in constant demand for "interpersonal giving." Societal demands on police officers were often beyond their ability to respond, which led to extreme frustration and subsequent suicide.

Heiman moved police suicide theory to a multidimensional orientation by calling for inclusion of psychological and social factors:

> A common sense approach would be to view police suicide from a psychological basis, emphasizing the unique and multidetermined aspects of suicide patterns, while at the same time being cognizant of the role of societal influences — man is a frustrated and status-oriented animal not isolated from his peers — at the individual-social interface. (Heiman, p. 273)

Gibbs and Martin (1964)

Gibbs and Martin (1964) theorized that suicide varies inversely with the degree of status integration in a population. They proposed that stable social relationships and status were important for psychological well-being. Heiman (1975) tested Gibbs and Martin's theory in a comparison between London bobbies and New York City police officers. He hypothesized that social acceptance of London bobbies is probably different than the "necessary evil" concept of American police officers. Thus,

London officers would have more stable social relationships and less suicides.

Loo (1986)

Loo (1986), in his study of Royal Canadian Mounted Police, conceptualized police suicide in terms of Baechler's (1979) framework. Baechler viewed suicide as a positive act of a relatively normal person struggling with life's problems and trying to resolve them. The focus of suicidal behavior is the person's personality, coping skills, and logic more so than the effects of society. Baechler provided four broad categories for the suicide act, including "escape" (flight, grief, self-punishment), "aggression" (vengeance, crime, appeal), "oblative" (sacrifice, transfiguration), and "ludic" (ordeal, game). Loo states that, based on his research, RCMP officers committed suicide as an "escape" function—that is, most of the officers committed suicide in response to life situations which were intolerable (p. 385).

Bonafacio (1991)

Bonafacio (1991) proposed a more recent psychodynamic approach to police suicide. Bonafacio agreed with other theorists that the effects of police work may be more than simply allowing aggression via a "license to kill." He hypothesized that feelings of helplessness may be brought on by the officer's exposure to crime, human misery, and death. These feelings may in turn exacerbate feelings of inadequacy that were already present in the officer's personality, causing overwhelming feelings of self-loathing.

Suicide may be the officer's attempt to restore feelings of strength and adequacy. Suicide in this regard is a demonstration of strength, courage, and mastery:

> As officers are overcome by witnessing misery and human degradation about which they can do nothing, and when cynicism and alcohol are unable to manage these feelings of self-hatred or feeling impotent, then suicide may become the next and last coping device to restore some semblance of self-esteem. The act of dying by gunshot may be a sign of courage and therefore a restoration of his ego ideal. (Bonafacio, p. 171)

The police officer experiences powerlessness as a terrible blow to the self-image of hero, which in turn causes feelings of self-hate for failing to live up to this ideal. Bonafacio offers a second explanation for the motivation of self-destruction:

> Friedman's description of the "aggressive" policeman also provides a clue to the unconscious motivation for suicide in those officers for whom the street has been a source of great pleasure, so great that they have been unable to resist it. These men have been seduced by "la puta," by the gratification of their aggressive and sexual impulses in the street. For these officers who cannot let go of such intense pleasure, there are no ethical and moral restraints on either their impulses or their behavior. The street has overwhelmed their conscience. The straight life of family, saving money, paying bills, and taking out the garbage is rejected for the excitement and action of the street life. (Bonafacio, p. 172)

In some officers, there may be feelings that they can never return to the innocence of life before police work:

> Some officers feel they have gone over the emotional edge and cannot return to the more moral but less satisfied men they were before they went into the street. They may feel that they have become tainted forever and can reclaim their moral self-worth by killing off the uncivilized, impulse dominated men they have become. (Bonafacio, p. 172)

Bonafacio's consensus is that the officer's id has overwhelmed the ego's capacity to maintain a balance between external reality and the superego. The id is too powerful for the ego to restrain; thus the superego must rely on the harshest means possible to regain its position: the destruction of the bad, pleasure-seeking part of the self. In this way, suicide is the officer's desperate attempt to restore self-concept as moral and decent. The police officer's motive is to punish the self for abandoning morality. In paying the ultimate penance for surrendering to impulses, the police officer seeks to reclaim the superego's approval. It is the intrapsychic equivalent to infantry officers calling in artillery on their own position rather than allowing it to be overrun by the enemy.

Chapter Seven

A PROPOSED THEORETICAL MODEL: POLICE SUICIDE AND CONSTRICTED ROLE IDENTITY

The idea that the social environment impacts on suicide is a constant feature throughout much of the literature. The exact role, however, that social factors may play in suicide remains a subject of debate. Adam (1990) comments that social variables involved in suicide can be dichotomized between two points of view: (1) the "macro social" view that examines associations between suicide rates, behavior and social conditions, and (2) the "micro social" view that seeks to show how social environment affects the vulnerability of the individual to suicide. An understanding of suicide suggests that it is a complex interaction involving social factors, individual susceptibility, and eventual symptomatic behavior. Adam views social factors as increasing suicide potential by increasing individual vulnerability, precipitating factors which trigger suicidal behavior, and exposing individuals to precipitants.

A viable theory of police suicide should include the interactional processes which Adam proposes. The social influence of the police environment may indeed impact the psychological resources of police officers. Allen (1986), for example, stated that suicide within law enforcement is not an isolated act committed by a police officer but an option whose choice is demanded of forces within the psychosocial environment. Allen adds that the suicide process in police work cannot be determined simply by looking at the individual; one must also look at the purpose of suicide within the total pattern of the officer's life.

In this chapter, we propose a psychosocial model of police suicide. Our goal is to examine the impact of the police social system on psychological and social resources of police officers, with the premise that this system may constrict such resources to a point of rendering them inflexible. Under conditions of this constriction, the potential for suicide may increase as the officer attempts to deal with life and work problems.

THE PSYCHOLOGICAL BENEFIT
OF MULTIPLE SOCIAL ROLES

The fact that the "police role" is placed in a position of high importance has implications for the officer's ability to use other roles for the amelioration of stress. As officers are socialized into believing that the police role is the "best" role in life, they may limit their choice to that role in times of distress. Constriction to a specific police role may affect the self-representational cognitive structure of officers. This structure defines the self as having purpose and meaning in the social environment. When this meaning is somehow lost or the person becomes isolated from the social environment through role restriction, a potential risk for suicide may result (Turner & Roszell, 1994).

Thoits (1986) has argued that individuals conceptualize the cognitive self as a set of social identities. "Identities," as defined by Thoits, refer to assigned positions in the social structure accepted by the individual. Identities are important for self-definition; they give meaning and purpose to individual social worth. Thoits (1986) hypothesized that the *more* social identities a person has, the *less* potential that person will have for depression, psychological distress, or suicide. Her findings indicated that symptoms of distress varied inversely with the number of social identities, and that changes in identities over time are psychologically beneficial or harmful, depending upon the direction of change.

Thus, how much the individual has at stake when confronted by an identity challenging situation is thought to depend on the number of other identities that make up the self. Fewer identities may be associated with increased vulnerability to suicide, and a greater accumulation of identities represent a meaningful resource against such acts (Turner & Roszell, 1994, p. 198). For police officers, the social constriction into a single role, that of *police officer,* may limit the psychologically beneficial nature of being able to utilize many roles.

The notion that multiple social identities can be beneficial in preventing depression and suicide is also associated with what Thoits (1986) refers to as the "identity accumulation hypothesis." This idea postulates an inverse relationship between the commitment to a particular identity and the number of identities taken on by the individual. As the number of role identities increase, the person's commitment to any one role identity will also decrease. For police officers, the forceful adherence to the police role may render them unable to commit to any other role. This reduces their ability to take on other roles which may help to reduce stress, depression, and the possibility of suicide.

Linville (1987) described a similar construct called "self-complexity." This idea proposed that vulnerability to stress and perhaps suicide may be due, in part, to differences in the *complexity* of self-representations. "Self-complexity" involves a greater number of social identities and a clear distinction between these identities. The greater number and clarity of each identity prevents negative events from spilling over to other identities, allowing protection of the total self from being overwhelmed by psychological distress or depression.

Just how strongly police officers are impacted by constriction may depend to some degree upon the "psychological centrality" that the police role occupies in the life of the officer. Roseberg and Pearlin (1978) and Gecas and Seff (1990) posit that the more important self-representational roles are made to people, the more those representations will be impacted by life challenges. Stryker and Serpe (1982) have also suggested that individuals tend to organize multiple cognitive identities in relation to the social environment and place these identities in a "salience hierarchy." Salience refers to the level of commitment an individual has to each identity and determines the likelihood that a given identity will be invoked across different life situations. The more salient the identity, the greater will be the impact of a serious negative event on the psychological well-being of the individual.

In summary, we have stated that the strong social influence police milieu may lead to a constricted role identity for police officers. Officers are expected to behave in a certain prescribed role: that of a police officer. This leads to speculation that the police officer's cognitive self-representations are also constricted and that they lack flexibility in moving to other life roles. As a consequence, police officers tend to deal with most life situations, good or bad, from the standpoint of their work role. Such lack of flexibility and the absence of other role identities may be a psychological disadvantage to officers and increase their potential risk for suicide.

THE ACQUISITION OF CONSTRICTIVE POLICE IDENTITY ROLES

Police work is addictive to individuals who occupy its ranks. Just ask any officer and they will tell you: "You become the job and the job becomes you, police work is in your blood until the day you die." In my conversation with police spouses, I hear similar sentiments: "He is a different person than he was before he became a cop. I think he is married to the job, not me. He acts and thinks like a cop 24 hours a day." It is of additional interest that police officers have considerable difficulty in retiring from police work because they cannot adjust to a new life role (Violanti, 1992).

Our evaluation of all of this is that police officers cannot easily step out of the police role. They appear to have difficulty taking other life roles such as "father," "husband," "civilian," or "emotional person." The question to explore is why this is so and what possible consequences it may have for an increased potential for suicide. It is hypothesized that police work has a constrictive impact on role identity acquisition by officers enmeshed within the police system and that this constriction may be associated with increased vulnerability to psychological stress and depression. Increased risk for suicide may thus be a result of the lack of other social identities to turn to for amelioration of psychological pain.

The Concept of Constriction

The basis for our conceptual model of police suicide stems from the proposed relationship of cognitive constriction and suicide:

> Synonyms for constriction are a tunneling or focusing or narrowing of the range of options usually available to that individual's consciousness when the mind is not panicked into dichotomous thinking: either some specific total solution or nothing. . . . One of the most dangerous aspects of a suicidal state is the presence of constriction. . . . The penchant toward dichotomous thinking is commonly seen in the suicidal person. (Shniedman, 1986, pp. 139–140)

Shniedman adds that one essence of good adjustment is to be able to view frustrating life situations as existential dichotomies rather than black-and-white situations to be solved immediately. Adjustment to social frustration lies in the individual's ability to make discriminations along the continuum of "black-and-white" solutions. Those capable of making such distinctions are less likely to choose an ultimate solution of suicide.

In our view, the concept of cognitive constriction may be applied to the social environment of policing. Social forces can essentially constrict the individual into behavioral patterns and roles. We hypothesize that the police system constricts role choices, just as individuals cognitively constrict behavior choices.

In police work, social constriction equates to rigid role requirements. The role of *police officer* as prescribed by the police environment allows for little choice of direction and, similar to personal constriction, quite often looks for solutions based on *black-or-white* decisions. Once officers are socialized into the police role, they may tend to all perceive the majority of problems from a constricted perspective. Under such circumstances, officers in crisis may fall back onto socialized constrictive thinking and increase their potential for suicide.

THE POLICE ROLE CONSTRICTION MODEL

Constriction in a police identity role is likely the result of a complex interactive system involving society at large, formal and informal police organization, and individual relationships within the police structure. In this section we provide a theoretical model of police role identity constriction and its possible pathways to suicide. Figure 2 illustrates our model.

EXPLANATION OF THE MODEL

The Formal Police Organization

The first link in police role identity constriction may be found in relationship between society and the formal police organization. The police organization may be viewed as an entity operating in a larger social system and, as such, is strongly influenced by that system. Police behavior is constrained and shaped by others in the system: judicial decisions, legislation, the media, and special-interest groups all work to limit the arbitrary power of the police. In response to outside systemic influence, the police organization attempts to adjust in order to preserve its own autonomy. Part of that adjustment involves strategies regarding organizational design, controlling the behavior of organizational members, and promoting a positive image of police (Violanti, 1981).

Problematic for the police organization, however, are the rapid changing demands of the larger social system. The police entity cannot possibly predict or continually adjust in the direction of such change. The

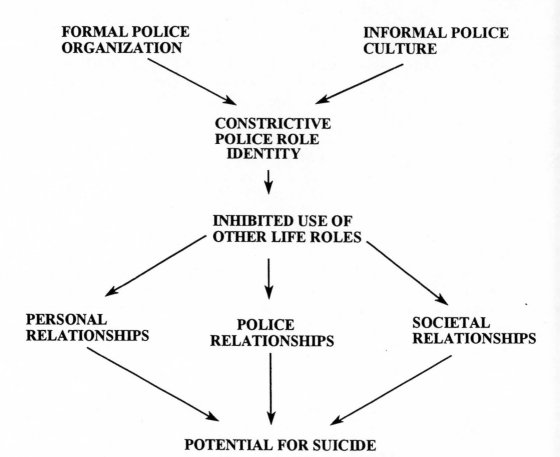

Figure 2. A Psychosocial Role Theory of Police Suicide.

typical response is to establish a rigid police organizational structure, which dictates explicit organizational roles and patterned interaction with the system. Rigid structure additionally provides strong control over the behavior of individual officers, deemed necessary to protect the police image.

Common in police structures are military-style rank positions, specific work roles, and impersonal work relationships. The police organization is unique from others because of the *intensity* with which it restricts officers—intensity resulting from rather powerful combinations of militaristic and bureaucratic control methods. The typical police organization may be said to "compound the felony" against officers in terms of control (Gross, 1970): they are coerced to behave consistent with the police role in a continuously changing environment and punished when they do not conform. Outstanding in police structure is the emphasis on rules and regulations. For the police organization, rules provide a symbolic guidance, a structure for the high frequency of interaction between officers and civilians. In essence, police officers are locked into the police role by the organization.

Effect on Individual Officers

Thus the police organization, in response to societal demands, attempts in various ways to adjust both its policies and the behavior of its individual officers. Such actions, however, affect the well-being of individual officers. First, prescribed organizational roles tend to constrict officers into rigid behavior patterns which diminish the ability of officers to take on other role identities. Secondly, the organization puts the individual officer on defense by what Kirschman (1983) termed the "deflection of blame": a form of individual control that protects the police organization at the psychological expense of its members. Blame deflection occurs when there is a threatening intrusion from the outside system that has the potential to reveal covert actions which may be detrimental to the image of the organization.

A third factor is organizational role expectation. Not only does the police organization demand rigid specific roles, it additionally prescribes how the officer must fulfill these roles. One result is what Harris (1973) called "false personalization": a facade of behavior expected to be seen in officers. False personalization forces officers to act out roles which in many cases are contrary to their true identities and feelings; it may call for superhuman individuals who are unaffected by anything that police work can throw at them. Kirschman (1983) speaks of an "occupational persona":

> One way to obfuscate occupational strain is to create an occupational persona, a mask of competence that belies one's actual state of mind. . . . It becomes harmful only when the inherent deception becomes a substitute for reality and is ultimately more acceptable than one's genuine, yet imperfect self. It is then that individual needs synchronize with organizational and cultural elements, and the officer's vulnerability to job stress is increased. . . . (p. 340)

In essence, officers who occupy the role of false persona or personalization may fail to attend to their true psychological self-representations. They forsake themselves and other role identities for those prescribed by the standards of the police organization.

The Informal Police Culture

The formal police organization is not alone in isolating officers into specific police role identities. The informal police culture places additional pressure on officers to conform to a distinct *police* role, but for different purposes. The informal police culture seeks to bond together officers against what it considers the evils of the world. This close-knit culture prescribes a theme of solidarity among officers which appears to help them deal with rejection from the greater society. Quite often, however, formal and informal police cultures are at odds with each other, and informal norms may regard police administration as the enemy. This seems to be a reaction to the rigid structure and role requirements of the formal organization. As a result, the informal police culture may become cohesive, setting up its own defense against society as well as the police administration.

The informal police culture has its own role requirements and there is a strong pressure to conform. First and foremost is loyalty; an officer never "rats" on another officer, and the code of secrecy remains very real and influential. Brown (1981) describes the value of loyalty in the informal police culture:

> As one patrolman expressed the matter, "I'm for the guys in blue! Anybody criticizes a fellow copper that's like criticizing someone in my family; we have to stick together." The police subculture demands unstinting loyalty to other officers, and receives, in return, protection and honor; a place to assuage real and imagined wrongs inflicted by a hostile public; safety from aggressive administrators and supervisors; and emotional support.... (Brown, p. 82)

At first glance, one might surmise that the police subculture is protective rather than detrimental to psychological health. While this may be true to some degree, the police subculture ultimately places the officer in a dilemma of role identity. To be accepted by the culture, the officer must, in essence, conform to the rather strict norms of loyalty prescribed by the group. In doing so, however, the officer must sacrifice individuality:

> The fusion of individual and group identity can be a powerful psychological aid for those who derive their self-esteem from group membership ... or it can be fraught with psychological terror for those whom fusion represents suffocation or the usurping of a feeble or formless identity. It can also represent a threat for those for whom distinction and achievement are synonymous with self-esteem.... (Kirschman, p. 280)

The strong push for cohesion by the informal police culture makes it constrictive in nature. Officers are often pulled in different directions as they attempt to conform to police cultural, organizational, and individual roles. It appears that the strength of formal and informal role requirements may place officers in a role-conflict situation. Regardless, both formal and informal police organization demand rigid identity roles from officers and often leave them with few alternatives.

THE IMPACT OF POLICE ROLE CONSTRICTION

The next part of our model concerns the effect of role identity constriction on the officer's ability to deal with stressful social interaction, both inside and outside of police work. It is hypothesized that social and interpersonal interactions may precipitate many of the risk factors associated with suicide, and the police officer's inability to be role-flexible in dealing with these interactions may increase the risk of suicide.

Interpersonal Relationships

Previous research has indicated that problems with interpersonal relationships may be a risk factor in suicide. Robin's (1981) account of the detailed case histories of 134 suicides, for example, is filled with accounts of difficulties in interpersonal relationships prior to the final suicidal act. Conroy and Smith (1983) reported that 18 of 19 suicide cases involved a significant family loss such as estrangement from family members, death of significant others, or divorce or separation issues between spouses. Jacobson and Portuges (1978) examined the relation of marital separation and divorce to suicide. They found that suicide potential is a significant issue in persons undergoing marital separation or divorce. Among the recently divorced, difficult transactions between spouses also increased suicide potential. Inter-spouse aggression was also associated with suicide. Much of the evidence would seem to indicate that interpersonal difficulties that precede suicides are not merely the result of transient conflict but part of a more pervasive and long-standing difficulty with relationships (Adam, 1990).

Personal Relationship Problems

Police officers as a group appear to have many problems with relationships, and previous research has shown that such problems may increase the potential for suicide. Ivanoff (1994), in her study of New York City police suicides, found that relationships were a primary factor in many police suicides over the past ten years. Her data suggested that 57.6 percent of police suicides from 1985–1994 involved personal relationship problems. Officers were involved in extramarital affairs, were recently separated or divorced, or had conflict with supervisors at work.

One reason for relational difficulties may be a police role-related emotional detachment from others. The role of a police officer calls for depersonalization; interpersonal relationships, on the other hand, call for human emotion. Police officers are socialized into not feeling emotion, to put up an emotional barrier to protect themselves from the human misery they witness. When officers are off-duty, however, they cannot turn their emotions back on. They remain stuck in prescribed "tough guy" roles that are seen as necessary to be an effective police officer. As a result, the personal relationships of police officers are not *personal* at all; they are more like a transaction on the street. Significant others soon become less important to the police officer. Compassion is subdued in favor of the police role, which takes precedent over most other emotional feelings. In some respects, the police role becomes a safe place to hide but at the same time does not allow for an outlet of emotions. The inability for police officers to move out of the constrictive police role to a role of family person, friend, or lover may be behind many police relationship problems. Reiser (1974) comments:

> Because the young officer tends to become overly immersed in the police role, communication at home may tend to break down. Distancing occurs between officer and spouse as the officer feels compelled to spend time with police peers. . . . (p. 40)

In true fashion of police role maintenance, attempts by police departments to provide assistance to officers and their families who have marital problems appear to focus on changing the spouse and not the officer. Through the use of education, departments try to impress on spouses that police work is difficult and that the spouse should be supportive of officers (Bonafacio, 1991). To the department, the police role is unchangeable; it is others outside the role who must adjust.

The cases outlined below are examples of police officers who were experiencing relationship problems and committed suicide.

> *Case 1.* This case involved two police officers who worked together in the same precinct. Both were involved in bitter disputes with their wives. One officer shot himself in the left temple as he sat alone in his house, a few days after his first anniversary on the force. The other

officer, a nine-year veteran, was described as outgoing and always "goofing around and cracking jokes." Six months before his death, the officer promised his wife that if she went to a marriage counselor he would kill himself. During an argument with her, the officer put his unloaded off-duty revolver to his head and twice pulled the trigger. When she ignored him, the officials said, he put one bullet in the chamber of his revolver and put the gun to his head. He pulled the trigger and the gun fired, sending a fatal bullet into his head.

Case 2. This officer, 24 years of age, had recently broken up with a girlfriend, but did not seem disturbed. The night of his death, he had been drinking all night with friends, and when he got into a car to leave, he put his gun to his head and threatened to pull the trigger. But some friends told investigators he had done the same thing several times before, and they thought he was just fooling around. One woman in the group, they said, took him seriously that night, however, and tried to grab the gun. It went off and he died.

Case 3. This case involved a chief of police, 62 years of age. The suicide was thought to result because of recent marital problems and a change in work assignment. The chief entered police headquarters at 6:15 A.M. and locked himself in his office. He then took out his police firearm and shot himself in the right temple. A handwritten note was scrawled beneath a memorandum that instructed the chief to take over a new assignment, an assignment which he considered punishment.

The motivation for suicide in these cases included a breakdown of intimate relationships due to the inability to assume roles other than the police role.

Police Peer Relationships

Constriction of personal identity into the police role may also affect relationships with police peers. As previously mentioned, loyalty and cohesiveness are important expectations of the police role, and those who violate the unwritten code of police brotherhood may pay the high price of rejection by the group. Thus, maintenance of police pride becomes an imperative and may pervade all aspects of the officer's life. To degrade or bring shame upon the police occupation becomes a moral trespass and may increase the potential for suicide.

Emphasis on the importance and constriction of the police role may lead to what Durkheim (1966) termed *altruistic* suicide. Altruistic suicide may be the result of officers' identities being so constricted to the police role that, for the good of the group, they commit suicide. In such a situation, officers may view themselves as counting little; it is the group that is paramount and interest is subordinated to the group. Police suicides based on shame or inability to fulfill role expectations of the organization, police peers, the public, or oneself indicates a strong symbolic identity between officers and the police role.

Altruistic suicide is the product of insufficient individuality and may be more common in occupations like police work where individuals tend to lose their own distinctive existence. The military is one example:

> Altruistic suicide is the product of insufficient individuation and is therefore more common in primitive societies (i.e., the military) where the individual has no clear sense of his own distinctive existence and is therefore ready to sacrifice himself for the group. For the same reason this form of suicide is a feature of military life, particularly in elite regiments with strong esprit de corps. (Campbell 1981)

Another example of altruistic suicide were Japanese Samurai warriors who participated in the practice of hara-kiri:

> The samurai was devoted to the code of chivalry and lived for the cause of honor, according to his own lights. To have his own name besmirched was the supreme stultification to the warrior. As he tried to live with honor, so his superiors tried to accord him an honorable method of death when his crime was not a dishonorable one. . . . If the hour comes, he is prepared for death and gravely faces an ordeal which early training has robbed of half its horrors. (Seward, 1968, p. 12)

Below are several cases of police suicide which involved thoughts of bringing dishonor to the role of police officer.

Case 1. This officer was 30 years of age and an eight-year veteran of the force. He left a note saying he was sorry if he had embarrassed anyone. The officer was found shortly before 7 a.m. on Tuesday by fellow officers after he failed to show up for work. His gun had been taken away and he had been assigned to the desk job after he became a suspect in a drug scandal. Though implicated in the inquiry, he was not charged with wrongdoing. The officer was found slumped in a car on a street outside a cemetery near his home. He had killed himself by placing the barrel of a .22-caliber rifle in his mouth and pulling the trigger. One of the officer's best friends stated that waiting for the disposition of the scandal had been agonizing for the officer. He said his friend's sense of himself was bound up in being a police officer.

Case 2. This suicide involved an officer who was thirty years old and a recent graduate of the police academy. Two days after graduating from the police academy and a day after being assigned to a precinct, the officer became intoxicated and struck another car, slightly injuring two people. Instead of stopping, he sped off and later reported his car stolen. New officers are on probation for their first two years, and the charges would have been enough to end the officer's career. He apparently shot himself in the chest with a handgun in his basement apartment amid empty beer cans. Nearby was a display of his uniform and his equipment set up in such a way that one official described it as "a shrine to the police department". He left a note apologizing to his parents and the department for any disgrace he might have brought them.

Case 3. This officer, 24 years of age and on the force for two years, had recently gotten into trouble by driving the wrong way on a one-way street and striking another car. No one was seriously injured, but the officer was worried that he would lose his job. After a day of drinking with friends, he walked into the street, put a gun in his mouth and pulled the trigger.

Case 4. This police officer, 26 years of age and on the department for 18 months, was recently fired after being charged with sexual assault. The officer was being pursued by a police patrol car. He drove his car to a freeway, stopped in the middle of rush hour traffic, took out his gun and began to fire shots into the air. He then stripped off his clothes and climbed onto a bridge railing. The officer then placed his firearm to his head and pulled the trigger.

Case 5. This case involved a chief of police, 62 years of age. The suicide was thought to result because of recent marital problems and a change in work assignment. The chief entered police headquarters at 6:15 a.m. and locked himself in his office. He then took out his police firearm and shot himself in the right temple. A handwritten note was scrawled beneath a memorandum that instructed the chief to take over a new assignment, an assignment which he considered punishment.

Case 6. A Japanese police superintendent, age 59, who was embarrassed by the failure of his officers to solve a major case, doused himself with kerosene and then burned himself to death. Prior to his death, the superintendent publicly apologized after his officers failed to make arrests in the case.

In the above cases, officers either left notes or in some way mentioned prior to the suicide that they were sorry they embarrassed the job. One officer went so far as to construct what was described as a "shrine" to the police department prior to his suicide. Others were embarrassed for such things as scandals, failure at performing their jobs properly, or being fired.

Police peers likely contributed to feelings of shame and guilt. Statements found in suicide notes like "I let the guys down" confirm the need of officers to fulfill their role identity. One might speculate that the potential for suicide is the result of a perceived unforgivable offense against the police role and the job. In a sense, the officer may have died for the corps.

Societal Relations

Individual police officer relationships with the society at large are also affected by role identity constriction. Police officers, because of the nature of their job, may become isolated from family, friends, and the general society. Experience in police work leads officers to perceive a dichotomous relationship between society and themselves; *society* is anyone who is not a police officer—they are the enemy and the *police* are the protectors of justice. Thus, police officers in their role purposely isolate themselves from society. Most social activities revolve around police organizations, and only other officers are considered *true* friends.

It has been argued that isolation is an important causal agent in suicide (Durkheim, 1952; Trout, 1980). Both Maris (1969) and Giddens (1971) agree that the principal variable linking psychological with social views of suicide is the isolation of the person from significant relationships. Suicide, according to Durkheim (1952), is based on a lack of societal integration. This integration works through two mechanisms: attachment and regulation. Durkheim argued that suicides can be classified in terms of the nature of an individual's integration into the social fabric. Without this attachment and regulation, individuals lack ties to the social order and the rules that govern it. This leaves them susceptible to suicide:

> Suicide varies inversely with the degree of integration of social groups of which the individual forms a part. The more weakened the groups to which he belongs, the less he depends on them, the more he consequently depends only on himself and recognizes no other rules of conduct than what are founded on private interest. If we agree to call this state egoism, in which the individual ego asserts itself to excess in the face of the social ego and at its expense, we may call egoistic the special type of suicide springing from excessive individualism. . . . Egoistic suicide is more frequent in modern, organic systems which reveal higher degrees of individual autonomy. (Turner & Beeghly 1981)

Campbell states:

> When people lose their sense of belonging to a group and become out of touch with the form that the group gives to their lives, they lose their own identity, their sense of place, their commitment to what they believe to be worthwhile

activities and so any realistic hope of a meaningful existence. This is the condition of anomie. . . . (1981, p. 149)

Police officers enmeshed in the police role identity may therefore lose psychological attachment to societal social groups and the goals of those groups. The potential for suicide is increased under such conditions.

CONCLUSION

To sum up, police suicide may in part be attributed to the nature of the police role and its constrictive effect on individual identity. The social power of formal and informal police organization rigidifies that role and leaves little alternative for the officer. Socially enforced adherence to the police role appears to lead to a constricted police identity, which limits the officer's cognitive and social flexibility in dealing with adversity or stress. Thus, police work may deprive officers of their ability to be flexible in life roles and relationships and, in doing so, place them into constricted psychological states which increase suicide potential.

Not all police officers are negatively affected and not all police suicides may be attributed to police role constriction. It is likely that the interaction of multiple factors come into play in the police suicide, including personality, present and past life experiences, prior socialization, and psychological disposition. With our proposed model, we are simply adding one more possible suicide potentiator to the already long list attributed to police work.

Chapter 8

POLICE SUICIDE PREVENTION

THE PROBLEM OF DENIAL

Initiating police suicide prevention programs in police work may prove to be a difficult task. Part of the problem stems from a strong sense of denial among police persons that suicide is a serious problem. Denial is likely based on the socialization of officers into a perception of superhuman emotional and survival control. From the first day in the police academy, officers are told that they are someone unique, far different from the average citizen and certainly beyond harm. This pervasive *illusion* of invulnerability seems to be prevalent among officers and is similar to Burger and Burns' (1988) concept of *unique invulnerability* found in adolescents. A component of this concept is the *personal fable,* a feeling that one is unique and has feelings and experiences unlike any other person. This feeling is reinforced by a strong belief in one's indestructibility (Greening & Dollinger, 1992).

Because of perceptions of invulnerability, entire departments may learn to deny feelings towards emotionally charged situations. Such is the case with the suicide of a peer officer. Violanti, Vena, Marshall, and Petralia (in press), for example, found that approximately 20 percent of police suicides were misclassified as either accidents or undetermined cause of death. Police investigators at the scene of a peer officer's suicide can effectively control (and explicitly deny) information about the suicide and lead medical examiners to consider other causes of death. Another example concerns a recent survey conducted by Susan Sawyer (personal communication, 1995), chairperson of C.O.P.S. (Concerns of Police Survivors). Ms. Sawyer sent requests for information on suicide to 14,000 police departments throughout the United States in an effort to help survivors. Only *three* departments responded!

ASSESSING SUICIDE RISK

Although any list of potential suicide risk factors is inconclusive, there are some indicators which may be associated with increased risk. Ivanoff and Tighe (1994) point out that there exists no profile of the "suicidal police officer," but that officers who may exhibit at least some warning signs should be given help. Essentially, there are five key characteristics which may identify the potential suicide victim (Lester, 1986, 1989):

1. *Age, race and sex* — males 50 years and older are at highest risk, while white females of any age at lowest risk. White males have the highest suicide rate of all demographic groups.

2. *Psychiatric symptoms* — persons with clinical depression are at highest risk for suicide. Depression is likely the most common warning sign of suicide, followed by those exhibiting symptoms of schizophrenia such as disorganization, confusion, chaos, and hallucinations. Least at risk are those with psychosomatic illnesses such as asthma and ulcers.

3. *Stress* — recent stress including daily hassles, life events, and traumatic events. Examples are a recent job loss, significant other or illness. The experience of a traumatic incident may also precipitate suicide. The number of stressful encounters is important; the more events that occur in a given time span, the more likely the possible consequence of suicide.

4. *Prior suicidal thoughts/attempts* — a person's potential for suicide is higher if they have had previous suicide attempts, have been considering suicide as an option, if they have specific plan and means readily available, and if a truly lethal means is contemplated (e.g., a police officer who always has a gun readily available). Each attempt increases the likelihood of success.

5. *Available resources* — a person who is isolated or has no means of social support has a greater risk for suicide, as is someone whose friends and family are openly hostile and rejecting. How helpful are the person's fellow officers, family, friends, and therapist? Is a safe, confidential place available for the officer to go for help?

A RECENT PREVENTION EFFORT:
THE NEW YORK CITY POLICE SUICIDE PROJECT

In 1994, twelve New York City police officers committed suicide. As a result of these tragic deaths, the New York City Police Foundation initiated a project to examine alternatives for suicide prevention. This project was an effort to develop a program which increased awareness and response to the problems leading to police suicide (Ivanoff, 1994b). As part of the project's effort, a video entitled *By Their Own Hand,* produced by Jonathan David, was introduced into a training program in the police department. The video depicted the suicide of three New York City police officers and the circumstances leading to those suicides.

The goal of the project was to initiate *prevention* as well as *intervention* for police suicide. As Ivanoff and Tighe (1994) suggest, prevention has been all but ignored in police work, while some attempts have been made towards intervention. Prevention of police suicide may, in essence, incorporate intervention as part of the total process.

Prior to the development of the program, Ivanoff (1994) conducted a study of New York City police officers concerning knowledge of suicide, experience with suicides, attitudes towards help-seeking, and possible reasons for suicide. Ivanoff asked officers to rank factors in police suicide and found the following (in descending order):

Ranked Factors in Police Suicide
(Responses of New York City Police Officers)

1. *Depression*
2. *Relationship conflicts or losses*
3. *Access to firearms*
4. *Drug/alcohol abuse*
5. *Financial difficulties*
6. *Involvement in corruption investigations*
7. *Difficulty with police organization*

Ivanoff also found that:

1. *About 25 percent of the officers surveyed knew someone in the department who they perceived as suicidal.*
2. *There was strong reluctance to seek help from inside or outside the department.*
3. *Police officers who participated in suicide awareness training stated that it helped to make them more aware of serious problems in themselves and other officers.*
4. *Results suggested that suicide awareness training contributed to improved attitudes and possible increased seeking of help.*

5. *Fewer police officers acknowledged suicidal ideation (24%) than persons in the general population (40%).*

Although stress, traumatic incidents, or access to firearms may be precipitants to police suicide, these factors cannot be significantly changed. Ivanoff therefore suggests that suicide prevention efforts focus on identifying *factors that can be changed,* such as knowledge and identification of risk factors and attitudes towards seeking help with personal problems.

The New York City project concluded that training in suicide awareness and help-seeking appeared to be useful for police officers. Training should begin at the police academy level to prevent the development of negative attitudes about seeking help for personal problems that may precipitate suicide. In addition, alternative *confidential* help resources should be developed in departments.

Suicide prevention involves getting help for officers who need it long before suicide feels like an option. Suicide does not just happen; it is the endpoint of a long and painful path of unendurable psychological pain. Intervention should thus be initiated on three levels: peer, supervisory, and administrative. Each of these levels should be evaluated separately as well as together to determine effectiveness (Ivanoff, 1994). A positive result of the New York City police suicide project was the subsequent development of a suicide training protocol for police officers (Ivanoff & Tighe, 1994).

A POLICE SUICIDE PREVENTION MODEL

Because suicide is likely the result of a complex interaction of many factors, all major components of the work environment must necessarily be involved in its prevention. Braverman (1995) pointed out that prevention in the work place goes far beyond initial screening and profiling of individuals employed. Instead, one should focus on systemic-level assessment of risk and development of policies and procedures to mitigate potential problems. Loo (1986) and Silverman and Felner (1995) comment that a suicide prevention approach should focus on suicide as well as building a person's work and life competencies, thereby enhancing their resilience to stressors. It must also be realized that suicide can result not from a single major crisis but from the accumulation of apparently minor life events (Loo, 1995).

The following is a proposal for a suicide prevention model readily adaptable to most police organizations. Police psychologists and others who work with police officers are cautioned about the primary purpose of a suicide prevention program: to assist the individual officer. Such programs, once implemented, tend to become entangled in organizational bureaucracy and may lose sight of this important goal.

Psychological Assessment

Although recruit screening in most major police departments involves psychological testing, quite often other personal and social factors are not considered. Loo (1995), for example, states that predisposing personality factors or precipitating family history (family violence, substance abuse) should be noted for tracking high-risk officers in the future. For officers already on the force who are being selected for special duty (SWAT teams, undercover, etc.), additional psychological assessment should be made to determine their suitability for such assignments. Loo (1995) suggests that officers on special assignments should be periodically evaluated for symptoms of distress, depression, or suicidal ideation. He also suggested that officers involved in critical incidents such as shootings be psychologically assessed.

Tracking High-Risk Officers

Loo (1995) has suggested that police departments develop criteria to identify and track high-risk officers (e.g., officers with marital difficulties, substance abuse, work problems, and other life problems) so that timely support can be provided prior to suicide. A behavior profile based on these indicators should be established for each officer and should be reviewed every six months to determine which officers are possibly at risk. Consultation with mental health professionals is essential when a police officer exhibits inappropriate behavior or behavioral change that suggests potential suicide. Other factors to consider are the personality structure and coping style of the police officer, depression, substance abuse, personality or anxiety disorders, or financial problems, physical illness, and problems with work. Past history of suicide attempts is also a very important factor to consider. There should be documentation of changes in behavior and problems of officers (McCafferty et al., 1992).

A working example of tracking is employed by the New York City Police Department's early intervention support group. Counselors assess a number of "points" for different types of problems that officers request help with. Points are weighted according the seriousness of the officer's problem. When officers get too high an accumulation of points, they are offered additional professional help.

Access to Firearms

Certainly, the risk of suicide increases in police officers because they have access to firearms. This author's data revealed that 95 percent of police suicides were by firearm (Violanti, in press). The practice of some departments requiring police to carry firearms off-duty may be an important target for police organizational policy change, as such required immediate access can facilitate impulsive suicidal tendencies in officers. Reducing access may work because suicidal impulses are often quite transitory. Persons whose preferred method of suicide is not available often do *not* resort to other means. Browning (1974) found that only about 10 percent of firearm suicides were performed by firearms purchased specifically for that purpose. The other 90 percent were committed by firearms already available to the person. There are some questions as to the necessity for officers to carry a firearm off-duty. While a firearm may certainly be necessary in life-or-death off-duty emergencies, police officers may seldom use their guns for such purposes. An informal survey of four large-sized urban police departments by the present researcher indicated that none of them kept statistical records of off-duty use of firearms by police officers.

Family Involvement

Seminars should be given for police recruits and their families so they understand the effects of police work. Marital problems can be a most significant stress-producing factor in the suicidal police officer. The police department may become the "mistress" of the officer and competition for the officer's spouse (McCafferty et al., 1992). Ivanoff (1994), for example, found that 58 percent of police suicides in New York City were the result of relationship problems with family or significant others. Counseling services should be made available to families and officers.

Training

Important for prevention is training which can help officers recognize and avoid psychological factors leading to suicide. Training should begin at the police academy level *before* new officers are exposed to the powerful effects of police occupational socialization. Training upon entrance is, in effect, an inoculation against future psychological crises and suicidal ideation (DeAngelis, 1993; Ivanoff, 1994). Ivanoff (1994) suggests that police suicide training programs include recognition of psychological depression, communication skills, conflict resolution, and intimate relationship maintenance. Supervisors as well as line personnel should be trained to recognize the warning signs of suicide and suggest confidential referrals at the scene. Supervisors can be an important source of support to line officers having difficulties (Beehr, King, & King, 1990; Coyne & Downey, 1991; Etzion, 1984; Pearlin & Schooler, 1978).

Stress Awareness and Coping Skills

Stress awareness is a psychologically sound method to help individuals cope with stress. A well-rounded stress education program should include identification of stress, the value and techniques of physical exercise, benefits of proper nutrition, interpersonal communication methods, and coping styles. Stress awareness is important on the recruit level to make new members aware of potential problems they will face in the future. On the in-service level, instruction in coping strategies should take priority since these members have most likely been exposed to the effects of job stress. Stress education on the family level should include identification of the police function, problems commonly encountered in police marriages, methods for effective communication, and the family as a source of support.

Supervisory

Supervisors are equally susceptible to the negative effects of police work. Middle-line supervisors should be able to identify potential suicidal officers under their command. Suicide sensitivity training should allow the supervisor to detect workers who are adversely affected by stress, alcohol abuse, and other correlates of suicide. Responsibility for such detection should be incorporated into the role of the supervisor.

Executive

Executive-level training in suicide awareness is also important. Executives can play a very important role in supportive functions, including organizational change and assistance with line officer problems. "Support from the top" can give officers an impression that the organization cares. Also, executives are not immune to the effects of police work. They too have the potential for suicide.

Intervention

Not only can an effective intervention effort save officers' lives, but it can also safeguard agencies from the devastating effects of suicide. Agencies must move beyond the morbidity of the subject to develop effective suicide countermeasures. Traditionally, no matter what their problems, police officers refrain from asking for help. There are various reasons for this reluctance. Officers do not wish to appear weak or vulnerable in front of their peers. They perceive themselves as problem solvers and not persons with problems.

To facilitate officers in taking the first difficult step to intervention, the police organization should develop and increase accessibility to confidential psychological services. Essentially, officers need a safe place to go for help, out of administrative view. If police officers can approach such services without going through formal organizational channels, they will be more likely to seek help and less likely to commit suicide (Ivanoff, 1994). Because all police officers face similar challenges and pressures — regardless of the size of the agency in which they serve — every officer should have access to comparable counseling resources.

Crisis Intervention

Prior experience has demonstrated that easy accessibility is an important factor in the troubled person's decision to seek help. A 24-hour private phone service would provide such accessibility. This suicide hot line could be made available to any member of the department by means of an 800 exchange. A civilian answering service would accept calls anonymously and notify members of an early intervention program via a beeper system. The call would then be returned and the problem initially discussed over the phone. If further intervention is needed, an in-person contact can be made. This system can reach the greatest number of people with the least amount of cost while still maintaining confidentiality.

Peer Support

It is easier for troubled officers to talk to other police officers. Providing trained peer support persons for members would be important. These counselors would not be expected to be psychologists but support persons, primarily there as someone to talk to.

Professional Intervention

It is necessary to establish a professional network of psychologists and/or psychiatrists who are familiar with police problems. When troubled members are in need of such services, they can easily be referred.

Retirement Counseling

Retirement is not an easy transition for most people and it is even more difficult for police officers. Gaska (1980) calculated a 10-fold risk of Detroit police retirees over the general population. The cohesiveness of police officers and the "protection" that being part of the police culture provides is lost upon separation from police service (Violanti, 1992). Many officers do not have skills for other types of employment and are unprepared for retirement which generally occurs at a young age. Informational seminars and counseling should be made available to officers as early as five years prior to retirement. Spouses and other family members should be included in such seminars.

Research

Each police department is unique and has its own set of problems. It is therefore necessary to conduct research into the potential causes and precipitants of suicide on a departmental level.

The Psychological Autopsy

Conducting "psychological autopsies" (Litman, 1970) is an excellent method for determining circumstances that may lead to suicide. A psychological autopsy involves gathering historical information about each suicide from police reports, death certificates, and medical examiner reports. In addition, members of the family and friends of the deceased may be interviewed. Some factors to consider:

1. *Demographic information (age, marital status, religion, rank, assignment)*
2. *Family background of significance;*
3. *Service performance ratings;*
4. *Recent medical history;*
5. *Recent reprimands, trouble at work;*
6. *Recent citations and commendations;*
7. *Critical incident trauma (e.g., shootings)*
8. *Military service;*
9. *History of suicide in family;*
10. *Details of suicide (methods, time, location, site of wound, etc.);*
11. *Recent life stresses;*
12. *Recent interpersonal problems (social, family, work);*
13. *Mental health, alcohol problems;*
14. *Any significant changes in person shortly before death (life routines, personality, habits, etc.)*

Information on these variables may not be readily available in all cases. Interviews with significant others of the deceased must be conducted with sensitivity due to the devastating effect that suicide has on family and friends.

In addition to psychological autopsies, there is a strong need for empirical studies on police suicide. To date, there is no national study which allows for the generalization of police suicide findings studied at individual police departments.

Chapter Nine

SURVIVORS OF POLICE SUICIDE

O ne of the most distressing events in policing is the suicide of an officer. Officers have consistently rated the death of a police officer as the most devastating stressor in their work (Eisenberg, 1979; Violanti & Aron, 1994).

For survivors, the sudden or unexpected death of a loved one can be a traumatic life event (McFarlane, 1986; Murphy, 1984; Green, Wilson & Lindy, 1985; Green, Lindy, Grace & Gleser, 1989). Parkes (1993) found that the death of a loved one is often associated with anxiety states, panic syndromes, and depression. Raymond (1988) found that intrusive memories of violent death very often trigger psychological difficulties in survivors. Survivors of line-of-duty military deaths often report psychological distress and trauma (Kirshner, 1982; Tyler & Gifford, 1990; Ursano, 1989). Amick-McMullin, Kilpatrick, Veronen, and Smith (1989) found that 66 percent of survivors had increased levels of psychiatric distress, prompted by dissatisfaction with the criminal justice system. Bard, Arnone, and Nemiroff (1985) found that PTSD symptoms existed among surviving family members of a homicide. Rynearson and McCreery (1993) found increased trauma symptoms in their sample of homicide survivors.

DIFFICULTIES FOR SUICIDE SURVIVORS

Although most duty-related deaths are distressful, suicide may create even more trauma for survivors. Danieli (1994) comments that suicide ruptures the family and exacerbates previous family ruptures. Kamerman (1993), in his study of New York City police suicides, concluded that these suicides adversely affected the lives of surviving wives, sons and daughters, grandchildren, and great-grandchildren. In addition to the immediate family, another group experiences the aftermath of suicide: police peers. There is often a grief wave in the department when an officer suicides. Police administrators have commented that somehow their officers do not seem the same after a suicide; supervisors notice an effect on morale, happiness and work. This emphasizes the need to recognize and prevent suicides among police personnel. Police leaders should arrange for psychological debriefings after the suicide of an officer that will help individual survivors and the department deal with the crisis. Discussed below are several reasons why suicides may be more difficult for police survivors to deal with than other types of death.

The Violent Nature of Suicide

The suicide of a police officer is usually of a violent nature; approximately 95 percent of police suicides involve a firearm (Violanti, in press). Such violence generally elicits strong emotional reactions from survivors, and a common reaction is that of anger towards the victim as well as the police organization. Family members may feel destructive, lash out at others, or even contemplate taking their own lives. Rudestam (1977) found survivors to be still quite angry at the deceased some seven months after the suicide.

Suddenness of Suicide

Suicide is usually sudden and unexpected. Suicide wreaks havoc among the survivors because the mind is simply not prepared for such a destructive event. A sudden suicide provides no warning, no prior anticipation, and no preparation. In addition, suddenness leaves the police survivor no time to work on unfinished relationship issues or to reach a sense of closure (Hauser, 1983).

Guilt

Suicide may engender guilt in survivors which may last for prolonged periods of time. Common statements of survivors are "I should have seen that there was a problem," or "part of this is my fault". Rudestam (1977), for example, found that 44 percent of suicide survivors still experienced guilt more than six months after the death.

Suicide and the System

Police suicide occurs in a system which is already replete with stress, and survivors are enmeshed within that system. Survivors will therefore have a more difficult time dealing with a suicide due to the multiple stressors they face.

Suicide and Mourning Rituals

Negative norms and perceptions evident in suicide deaths appear to spill over into police rituals. In most cases, for example, a full military funeral is not given to a police officer who commits suicide. Peers and administrators may feel uneasy with such a funeral, as suicide is considered more a shameful than heroic death.

Instead of support in cases of suicide, what appears to occur is avoidance, gossip, and cloaked communications. The family's sense of being different, isolated, and ashamed may be reinforced by negative reactions of police peers and administration toward the suicide (Calhoun, Selby, & Selby, 1982). One police widow told of how the department first blamed her for the death of her husband until investigation revealed that he had killed himself.

Communication Problems

Calhoun, Abernathy, and Selby (1986) found that in cases of suicide friends and family members found it more difficult to communicate with survivors. The authors concluded that there are strong norms for indicating *what not to do* in cases of suicide and suggest that suicide deaths tend to discourage meaningful interaction with survivors. Friends, for example, were extremely uncomfortable in asking about the cause of death, details of the death, or saying that the death was "best" for the deceased.

Shneidman (1972) observed that, from all varied modes of death, suicide brings the greatest stigma on survivors and produces greater discomfort in those who must act with family members. This has been termed "ambivalent avoidance" (Whitis, 1972). Danto (1977) found that the absence of support often reflects the stigma attached to the act of suicide. Argyle, Furnham and Graham (1981) suggest that the rules of interaction for with suicide survivors are more constraining that other forms of death. Judgments about the existence of social rules tend to be more inclusive and extreme in a "should not" direction when the death is a suicide. They suggested that although persons feel greater compassion for survivors of suicide, they may still avoid the situation for fear of violating one of the rules.

Abandonment by the Police Department and Peers

It is unfortunate that survivors of police suicide must not only deal with their own grief but also with negative reactions of police peers, the organization, and the public. The police work group has the *potential* to provide a supportive set of conditions in reducing psychological distress, since it provides environmental structure, leadership, companionship and a source of motivation for recovery (Figley, 1988). The extended "police family"—other officers, the police agency, and police benevolent groups, can reinforce a sense of understanding and recognition for the survivor (Williams, 1987).

Quite often, however, survivors of police suicide are abandoned more quickly than those of officers who died from other causes. Police officials may not place much emphasis on assisting survivors of police suicide due to the stigma associated with such deaths. Sawyer (1988) stated that officers dislike interacting with the widow of a slain officer because it · reminded them of their own vulnerability. Several researchers (Stillman, 1986, 1987; Sawyer, 1988) have admonished the police department and its members for abandoning the police spouse after the death of an officer. Interviews with police spouse survivors have supported the fact that the police network may not always be available. A police wife comments:

> My husband died on duty about two years ago. The department and all of his police friends were extremely helpful immediately after his death, but I have not seen them since. No one from the department or any officers have stopped at the house. I think I would be very pleased just to see any of them again. I felt abandoned and uncared for.

RESEARCH ON POLICE SURVIVORS

Little research is available which specifically explores the effects of police suicides on survivors. Danto (1975) conducted interviews with ten police widows from the Detroit Police Department and found that they reported weight loss, sleep difficulties, loss of interest in activities, and suicidal thoughts after the death. Likely the most comprehensive study to date on police survivors was conducted by Stillman (1986). Stillman measured psychological distress and trauma in police spouse survivors and found that more than 50 percent met the criteria for posttraumatic stress disorder after the death. Spouses demonstrated increased levels of depression, anxiety, hostility and guilt. Stillman pointed out that police deaths may be even more traumatic than deaths in other occupations due to the high visibility of police work. Police deaths may involve contingencies of the department, media, criminal justice system, and community. The death may have occurred in close proximity to or at the officer's residence, and the spouse may have to pass by the scene on a daily basis.

The Importance of Departmental and Peer Support

To demonstrate that police support is important after an officer's death, Violanti (1995) examined the effect of such support on psychological distress in police death survivors. Survivors reported that they experienced a high degree of both psychological distress and trauma as a result of their loved one's death. Stress symptoms decreased significantly when police friends, the department, and fraternal police groups offered support. This finding attested to the strong source of support associated with the police culture.

REFERENCES

Adam, K. S. (1990). Environmental, psychosocial, and psychoanalytic aspects of suicidal behavior. In S. J. Blumenthal & D. J. Kupfer (Eds.), *Suicide over the life cycle* (pp. 39–96). Washington, DC: American Psychiatric Press.

Aldridge, D., & St. John, K. (1991). Adolescent and pre-adolescent suicide in New-foundland and Labrador. *Canadian Journal of Psychiatry, 36,* 432–436.

Allen, S. (1986). Suicide and indirect self-destructive behavior among police. In J. Reese & H. Goldstein (Eds.), *Psychological services for law enforcement* (pp. 412–416). Washington, DC: US Government Printing Office.

Alpert, G. P., & Dunham, R. G. (1988). *Policing urban America.* Prospect Heights, Illinois: Waveland.

American Psychiatric Association. (1994). *Diagnostic and statistical manual of mental disorders* (4th Ed.). Washington, DC: APA, pp. 427–429.

Amick-McMullin, A., Kilpatrick, D. G., Veronen, L. J., & Smith, S. (1989). Family survivors of homicide victims: Theoretical perspectives and an exploratory study. *Journal of Traumatic Stress, 2,* 21–35.

Arato, M., Demeter, E., Rihmer, Z., & Somogyi, E. (1988). Retrospective psychiatric assessment of 200 suicides in Budapest. *Acta Psychiatry. Scand., 77,* 454–456.

Argyle, M., Furnham, A., & Graham, J. A. (1981). *Social situations.* Cambridge, MA: Cambridge University Press.

Aron, F. H. (1992). *An analysis of sources of police stress.* Unpublished master's thesis, Russell Sage College, Albany, NY.

Asgard, U. (1990). *Suicide among Swedish women: A psychiatric and epidemiologic study.* Stockholm: Kongl Carolinska Medico Institutet, (pp. 10–15).

Aussant, G. (1984). Police suicide. *RCMP Gazette, 46,* 14–21.

Baechler J. (1979). *Suicide.* New York: Basic Books.

Bard, M., Arnone, H. C., & Nemiroff, D. (1985). Contextual influences on the post-traumatic stress adaptation of homicide survivor-victims. In C. R. Figley (Ed.), *Trauma and its wake: Vol. 2. Traumatic stress theory, research, and intervention* (pp. 90–112). New York: Brunner/Mazel.

Barraclough, B. M. (1972). Are the Scottish and English suicide rates really different? *British Journal of Psychiatry, 124,* 526–530.

Barraclough, B. M. (1974). Poisoning cases: Suicide or accident. *British Journal of Psychiatry, 124,* 526–530.

Bayley, D. H. (1986). The tactical choices of police patrol officers. *Journal of Criminal Justice, 14,* 329–348.

Beehr, T., King, L., & King, D. (1990). Social support and occupational stress: Talking to supervisors. *Journal of Vocational Behavior, 36,* 61–81.

Beutler, L. E., Nussbaum, P. D., & Meredith, K. E. (1988). Changing personality patterns of police officers *Professional Psychology: Research and Practice, 19,* 503–507.

Bonafacio, P. (1991). *The psychological effects of police work.* New York: Plenum.

Braverman, M. (1995, September). *Beyond profiling: An integrated multidisciplinary approach to preventing workplace violence.* Symposium conducted at the Work, Stress and Health '95 conference, Washington, DC.

Brown, M. K. (1981). *Working the street: Police discretion and the dilemmas of reform.* New York: Russell Sage.

Browning, J. H. (1974). Epidemiology of suicide: Firearms. *Comprehensive Psychiatry, 15,* 549–553.

Burger, J. M., & Burns, L. (1988). The illusion of unique vulnerability and the use of effective contraception. *Personality and Social Psychology Bulletin, 14,* 264–270.

Calhoun, L. G., Selby, J. W., & Selby, L. E. (1982). The psychological aftermath of suicide: An analysis of current evidence. *Clinical Psychology Review, 2,* 490–420.

Calhoun, L. G., Abernathy, C. B., & Selby, J. W. (1986). The rules of bereavement: Are suicidal deaths different? *Journal of Community Psychology, 14,* 213–218.

Campbell, T. (1981). *Seven theories of human society.* New York: Oxford.

Centers for Disease Control. (1985). *Suicide surveillance 1970–1980.* Atlanta, GA: U.S. Department of Health and Human Services.

Centers for Disease Control. (1987). Postservice mortality among Vietnam veterans. *Journal of the American Medical Association, 257,* 790–795.

Centers for Disease Control. (1994). Firearm-related years of potential life lost before age 65 years—United States, 1980–1991. *CDC Morbidity and Mortality Weekly Report, 43,* 609–611.

Checkoway, H., Pearce, N. E., & Crawford-Brown, D. J. (1989). *Research methods in occupational epidemiology.* New York: Oxford University Press.

Conroy, R. W., & Smith, K. (1983). Family loss and hospital suicide. *Suicide and Life-Threatening Behavior, 13,* 179–194.

Coyne, J., & Downey, G. (1991). Social factors and psychopathology: Stress, social support and coping processes. *Annual Review of Psychology, 42,* 401–425.

Cronin, T. J. (1982). *Police suicides: A comprehensive study of the Chicago Police Department 1970–1979.* Master's thesis, Lewis University, Romeoville, Illinois.

Curran, P. S., Finlay, R. J., & McGarry, P. J. (1988). Trends in suicide. *Irish Journal of Psychological Medicine, 5,* 98–102.

Danieli, Y. (1994). Trauma to the family: Intergenerational sources of vulnerability and resilience. In J. T. Reese & E. Scrivner (Eds.), *Law enforcement families: Issues and answers* (pp. 163–176). Washington, DC: U.S. Government Printing Office.

Danto, B. L. (1975). Bereavement and the widows of slain police officers. In E. Shoenberg (Ed.), *Bereavement: Its psychological aspects* (pp. 150–163). New York: Columbia.

Danto, B. L. (1977). Crisis and death intervention: Recruitment, training, and supervision of the volunteer. In B. L. Danto & A. H. Kutscher (Eds.), *Suicide and bereavement* (pp. 240–248). New York: MSS Information Corporation.

Danto, B. L. (1978). Police suicide. *Police Stress, 1,* 32–35.

Dash, J., & Reiser, M. (1978). Suicide among police in urban law enforcement agencies. *Journal of Police Science and Administration, 6,* 18–21.

DeAngelis, T. (1993). Workplace stress battles fought all over the world. *APA Monitor, 24,* 22.

Douglas, J. (1967). *The social meanings of suicide.* Princeton, NJ: Princeton University Press.

Durkheim, E. (1952). *Suicide.* Glencoe, Illinois: Free Press.

Durkheim, E. (1966). *Suicide.* New York: Free Press.

Eisenberg, T. (1975). Job stress and the police officer: Identifying stress reduction techniques. In W. H. Kroes & J. J. Hurrell, Jr. (Eds.), *Job stress and the police officer: Identifying stress reduction techniques* (pp. 26–34) (HEW Publication No. NIOSH 76-187). Washington, DC: U.S. Government Printing Office.

Elkind, D. (1967). Egocentrism in adolescence. *Child Development, 38:* 1025–1034.

Ellison, K., & Genz, J. (1983). Stress and the police officer (p. 44). Springfield, IL: Charles C Thomas.

Etzion, D. (1984). Moderating effects of social support on the stress burnout relationship. *Journal of Applied Psychology, 69,* 615–622.

Farberow, N. L. (1980). *The many faces of suicide.* New York: McGraw-Hill.

Farberow, N. L., Kang, H. K., & Bullman, T. A. (1990). Combat experience and postservice psychosocial status as predictors of suicide in Vietnam veterans. *Journal of Nervous and Mental Disease, 178,* 32–37.

Federal Bureau of Investigation. (1990). *FBI uniform crime reports: Law enforcement officers killed and assaulted* (p. 40). Washington, DC: U.S. Dept. of Justice.

Figley, C. R. (1988). Toward a field of traumatic stress. *Journal of Traumatic Stress, 1,* 316.

Forastiere, F., Perucci, C. A., DiPietro, A., Miceli, M., Rapiti, E., Bargagli, A., & Borgia, P. (1994). Mortality among urban policemen on Rome. *Am. Journal of Industrial Medicine, 26,* 785–798.

Fowlie, D. G., & Aveline, M. O. (1985). The emotional consequences of ejection, rescue, and rehabilitation in the Royal Air Force crew. *British Journal of Psychiatry, 146,* 609–613.

Foy, D. W., Sipprelle, R. C., Rueger, D. D., & Carroll, E. M. (1984). Etiology of post-traumatic stress disorder in Vietnam veterans: Analysis of pre-military, military, and combat exposure influences. *Journal of Consulting and Clinical Psychology, 52,* 88–96.

Fridell, L. A., & Binder, A. (1992). Police officer decision making in potentially violent confrontations. *Journal of Criminal Justice, 20,* 385–399.

Friedman, P. (1968). Suicide among police: A study of 93 suicides among New York City policemen 1934–40. In E. S. Shneidman (Ed.), *Essays of self destruction* (pp. 414–419). New York: Science House.

Frye, J., & Stockton, R. A. (1982). Discriminant analysis of post traumatic stress among a group of Vietnam veterans. *American Journal of Psychiatry, 139,* 52–56.

Gaines, L., Southerland, M., & Angell, J. (1991). *Police administration.* New York: McGraw-Hill.

Gaska, C. W. (1980). *The rate of suicide, potential for suicide, and recommendations for prevention among retired police officers.* Doctoral Dissertation, Wayne State University.

Gecas, V., & Seff, M. A. (1990). Social class and self-esteem: Psychological centrality, compensation, and the relative effects of work and home. *Social Psychological Quarterly, 53,* 165–173.

Gibbs, J. P. (1961). Suicide. In R. K. Merton & R. Nisbet (Eds.), *Contemporary social problems.* New York: Harcourt, Brace & World.

Gibbs, J. P., & Martin, W. T. (1964). *Status integration and suicide: A sociological study.* Oregon: University of Oregon Press.

Giddens, A. (1971). *The sociology of suicide: A selection of readings.* London: Frank Cass & Company.

Graf, F. (1986). The relationship between social support and occupational stress among police officers. *Journal of Police Science and Administration, 14,* 178–186.

Green, B. L., Wilson, J. P., & Lindy, J. D. (1985). Conceptualizing PTSD: A psychosocial framework. In C. R. Figley (Ed.), *Trauma and its wake: The study and treatment of post-traumatic stress disorder* (pp. 53–69). New York: Brunner/Mazel.

Green, B. L., Lindy, J. D., Grace, M. C., & Gleser, G. C. (1989). Multiple diagnosis in post-traumatic stress disorder: The role of war stressors. *Journal of Nervous & Mental Disorders, 177,* 329–335.

Greening, L., & Dollinger, S. J. (1992). Illusions of invulnerability: Adolescents in a natural disaster. *Journal of Traumatic Stress, 5,* 63–75.

Gross, E. (1970). Work, organization, and stress. In R. Levine & C. Scotch (Eds.), *Social stress.* Chicago: Aldine.

Guralnick, L. (1963). *Mortality by occupation and cause of death among men 20–64 years of age* (Vital Statistics Special Reports, 53). Bethesda, Maryland: DHEW.

Hageman, M. (1978). Occupational stress and marital relationships. *Journal of Police Science and Administration, 6,* 407–412.

Harris, R. N. (1973). *The police academy: An inside view.* New York: Wiley.

Hauser, M. J. (1983). Bereavement outcome for widows. *Journal of Psychosocial Nursing and Mental Health Services, 21,* 22–31.

Hearst, N., Newman, T. B., & Hulley, S. B. (1986). Delayed effects of the military draft on mortality randomized natural experiment. *New England Journal of Medicine, 314,* 620–624.

Heiman, M. F. (1975). The police suicide. *Journal of Police Science and Administration, 3,* 267–273.

Heiman, M. F. (1977). Suicide among police. *American Journal of Psychiatry, 134,* 1286–1290.

Hendin, H., & Haas, A. P. (1991). Suicide and guilt as manifestations of PTSD in Vietnam combat veterans. *Am. Journal of Psychiatry, 148,* 586–591.

Henry, A., & Short, J. (1954). *Suicide and homicide.* Glencoe, IL: Free Press.

Hitz, D. (1973). Drunken sailors and others: Drinking problems in specific occupations. *Quarterly Journal on Studies in Alcohol, 34,* 496–505.

Holding, T. A., & Barraclough, B. M. (1978). Undetermined deaths—suicide or accident? *British Journal of Psychiatry, 133,* 542–549.

Hovanitz, C. A. (1986). Life event stress and coping style as contributions to psychopathology. *Journal of Clinical Psychology, 42,* 34–41.

Ivanoff, A. (1994). *The New York City police suicide training project* (pp. 5–15). New York: Police Foundation.

Ivanoff, A. (1994b, October). *Police suicide.* Testimony letter to New York City Committee on Civil Service and Labor.

Ivanoff, I., & Tighe, M. (1994). *Suicide and the police officer: Getting help before it is too late.* Training protocol, New York City Police Department.

Jacobson, G. F., & Portuges, S. H. (1978). Relation of marital separation and divorce to suicide: A report. *Suicide and Life-Threatening Behavior, 8,* 217–224.

Janik, J., & Kravitz, H. (1994). Police suicide: Troubles at home. In J. T. Reese & E. Scrivner (Eds.), *Law enforcement families: Issues and answers* (pp. 73–82). Washington, DC: U.S. Government Printing Office.

Josephson, R. L., & Reiser, M. (1990). Officer suicide in the Los Angeles police department: A twelve year follow-up. *Journal of Police Science and Administration, 17,* 227–229.

Kappeler, V. E., Blumberg, M., & Potter, G. W. (1993). *The mythology of crime and criminal justice* (pp. 134–136). Prospect Heights, Illinois: Waveland.

Kamerman, J. (1993). The illegacy of suicide. In A. A. Leenaars (Ed.), *Suicidology: Essays in honor of Edwin S. Shneidman* (pp. 346–355). New Jersey: Jason Aronson.

Kellerman, A. L., Rivara, F. P., Somes, G., Reay, D. T., Francisco, J., Banton, J. G., Prodzinski, J., Fligner, C., & Hackman, B. B. (1992). Suicide in the home in relation to gun ownership. *New England Journal of Medicine, 327,* 467–472.

Kelling, G., & Pate, M. (1975). The person-role fit in policing: The current knowledge and future research. In W. Kroes & J. J. Hurrell, Jr. (Eds.), *Job stress and the police officer: identifying stress reduction techniques* (HEW Publication no. [NIOSH] 76-187). Washington, DC: U.S. Government Printing Office.

Kessler, R. C. (1979). A strategy for studying differential vulnerability to the psychological consequences of stress. *Journal of Health and Social Behavior, 20,* 10–108.

Kirshner, E. (1982). Data on bereavement and rehabilitation of war widows. In C. D. Spielberger & I. G. Sarason (Eds.), *Stress and anxiety* (Vol. 8, pp. 219–224). New York: Hemisphere.

Kirsher, T., Nelson, J., & Burdo, H. (1985). The autopsy as a measure of the accuracy of the death certificate. *New England Journal of Medicine, 313,* 1263–1269.

Kirschman, E. (1983). *Wounded heroes: A case study and systems analysis of job-related stress and emotional dysfunction in three police officers.* Doctoral Dissertation, University Microfilms International, Ann Arbor, Michigan.

Kitsuse, J., & Cicourel, A. (1963). A note on the use of official statistics. *Social Problems, 11,* 131–139.

Kleck, G. (1988). Miscounting suicides. *Suicide and Life-Threatening Behavior, 18,* 219–236.

Kramer, M., Pollack, E., Reddick, R., & Locke, B. (1972). *Mental disorders/suicide.* Cambridge: Harvard University Press.

Kroes, W. (1986). *Society's victim: The police.* Springfield, Illinois: Charles C Thomas.

Labovitz, S., & Hagehorn, R. (1971). An analysis of suicide rates among occupational categories. *Sociological Inquiry, 41,* 67–72.

Langston, E. (1995, March). *Police suicide.* Presentation at American Criminal Justice Society Annual Conference, Boston, MA.

Laufer, R. S., Gallops, M. S., & Frey-Wouters, E. (1984). War stress and trauma: The Vietnam veteran experience. *Journal of Health and Social Behavior, 25,* 65–85.

Law Enforcement News (April, 1995). National FOP looks at police suicide and how to prevent it. 1–8.

Lazarus, R. S. (1981). The stress and coping paradigm. In C. Eisdorfer, D. Cohen, A. Kleinman, & P. Maxim (Eds.), *Models for clinical psychopathology* (pp. 177–214). New York: Spectrum.

Lennings, C. J. (1994, February). *Suicide ideation and risk factors in police officers and justice students.* Paper presentation at the Public Health Association Conference, Canberra, Australia.

Lester, D. (1986). The suicidal person: Recognition and helping. *Police Journal, 59,* 216–221.

Lester, D. (1989). Can we predict who will commit suicide? In D. Lester, *Questions and answers about suicide* (pp. 29–30). Philadelphia, PA: Charles Press.

Lester, D. (1992). Suicide in police officers: A survey of nations. *Police Studies, 15,* 146–148.

Lester, D. (1993). A study of police suicide in New York City, 1934–1939. *Psychological Reports, 73,* 1395–1398.

Linville, P. W. (1987). Self-complexity as a cognitive buffer against stress-related illness and depression. *Journal of Personality and Social Psychology, 52,* 663–676.

Litman, R. E., Curphey, T., Shneidman, E. S., Farberow, N. L., & Tabachnick, N. (1963). Investigations of equivocal suicides. *Journal of the American Medical Association, 184,* 924–929.

Litman, R. E. (1970). Sigmund Freud on suicide. In E. S. Shneidman, N. L. Farberow, & R. E. Litman (Eds.), *The psychology of suicide* (pp. 565–586). New York: Science House.

Loo, R. (1986). Suicide among police in a federal force. *Suicide and Life-Threatening Behavior, 16,* 379–388.

Loo, R. (1995, September). *Police suicide: Issues, prevention and postvention.* Poster session conducted at the Work, Stress and Health '95 conference, Washington, DC.

Mantell, M. R., & Dubner, J. S. (1988). *San Ysidro massacre: Impact on police officers.* San Diego, CA: Police Department Psychological Service Program.

Maris, R. (1969). *Social forces in urban suicide.* Homewood, IL: Dorsey Press.

Martelli, T., Waters, L., & Martelli, J. (1989). The police stress survey: Reliability and relation to job satisfaction and organizational commitment. *Psychological Reports, 64,* 267–273.

Martin, C. A., McKean, H. E., and Veltkamp, L. J. (1986). Post-traumatic stress disorder in police and working with victims: A pilot study. *Journal of Police Science and Administration, 14,* 98–101.

McCafferty, F. L., McCafferty, E., & McCafferty, M. A. (1992). Stress and suicide in police officers: A paradigm of occupational stress. *Southern Medical Journal, 85,* 233–243.

McCarthy, P. D., & Walsh, D. (1975). Suicide in Dublin: I. The underreporting of suicide and the consequences for national statistics. *British Journal of Psychiatry, 126,* 301–308.

McFarlane, A. C. (1986). Post-traumatic morbidity of a disaster: A study of cases presenting for psychiatric treatment. *J. Nerv. & Mental Dis., 174,* 4–13.

McMichael, A. J. (1976). Standardized mortality ratios and the healthy worker effect: Scratching beneath the surface. *Journal of Occupational Medicine, 18,* 165–168.

McNeill, J., Lecca, P., & Wright, R., Jr. (1983). *Military retirement: Social, economic, and mental health dilemmas.* New Jersey: Rowman and Allanhead.

Menninger, K. (1938). *Man against himself.* New York: Harcourt, Brace World.

Milham, S. (1979). *Occupational mortality in Washington state.* U.S. Dept. of Health, Education, and Welfare, 1–3. Washington, DC: U.S. Government Printing Office.

Moldeven, M. (1994). *Military-civilian teamwork in suicide prevention.* (pp. 3–51). Los Angeles, California: Moldeven.

Monk, M. (1987). Epidemiology of suicide. *Epidemiologic Reviews, 9,* 51–69.

Moyer, L., Boyle, C., & Pollock, D. (1989). Validity of death certificates for injury-related causes of death. *American Journal of Epidemiology, 130,* 1024–1032.

Murphy, G. E. (1992). *Suicide in alcoholism* (pp. 10–12). New York: Oxford Press.

Murphy, S. A. (1984). Stress levels and health status of victims of a natural disaster. *Res. in Nursing & Health, 7,* 205–215.

Nelson, Z., & Smith, W. E. (1970). The law enforcement profession: An incidence of high suicide. *Omega, 1,* 293–299.

New York State Dept. of Health. (1984). *Statistics on occupational deaths: Police officers.* Albany, N.Y.

Niederhoffer, A., & Niederhoffer, E. (1978). *The police family: From station house to ranch house* (pp. 50–65). Lexington: D.C. Heath.

Nielson, E. (1986). Understanding and assessing traumatic stress reactions. In J. T. Reese & H. Goldstein (Eds.), *Psychological services for law enforcement* (pp. 369–373). Washington, DC: U.S. Government Printing Office.

Nix, C. (1986). Police suicide: Answers are sought. *The New York Times,* September 15, B2–4.

O'Carroll, P. W. (1989). A consideration of the validity and reliability of suicide mortality data. *Suicide and Life-Threatening Behavior, 19,* 1–16.

O'Carroll, P. W., Rosenberg, M. L., & Mercy, J. A. (1991). Suicide. In M. L. Rosenberg & M. A. Fenley (Eds.), *Violence in America* (pp. 190–193). New York: Oxford University Press.

Parkes, C. M. (1993). Psychiatric problems following bereavement by murder or manslaughter. *British Journal of Psychiatry, 162,* 49–54.

Pearlin, L. I. & Schooler, C. (1978). The structure of coping. *Journal of Health and Social Behavior, 19,* 2–21.

Peck, D. L. (1984). Post-traumatic stress and life destructive behavior. *Journal of Sociology and Social Welfare, 10,* 15–21.

Perrier, D., & Toner, R. (1984). Police stress: The hidden foe. *Canadian Police Journal,* *8,* 15–19.

Pescosolido, B., & Mendelsohn, R. (1986). Social causation or construction of suicide? An investigation into the social organization of official rates. *American Sociological Review, 51,* 80–101.

Phillips, D. P., & Ruth, T. E. (1993). Adequacy of official suicide statistics for scientific research and public policy. *Suicide and Life-Threatening Behavior, 23,* 307–319.

Pogrebin, M. R., & Poole, E. D. (1991). Police and tragic events: The management of emotion. *Journal of Criminal Justice, 19,* 395–403.

Pokorny, A. D. (1967). Suicide in war veterans: Rates and methods. *Journal of Nervous and Mental Disease, 144,* 224–229.

Posner, M. (1995). Suicide tops the cause of police deaths. *Philadelphia Enquirer,* p. 4.

Rangell, L. (1967). The metapsychology of psychic trauma. In S. S. Furst (Ed.), *Psychic trauma.* New York: Basic Books.

Raymond, C. A. (1988). Study says memories of violent death linger in survivors, trigger psychological problems. *Journal of the American Medical Association, 259,* 3524–3529.

Reese, J. T. (1986). Policing the violent society: The American experience. *Stress Medicine, 2,* 233–240.

Reiser, M. (1974). Some organizational stressors on police officers. *Journal of Police Science and Administration, 2,* 156–159.

Rich, C. L., Young, D., & Fowler, R. C. (1986). San Diego suicide study: I. young vs. old subjects. *Archives General Psychiatry, 43,* 577–582.

Richard, W., & Fell, R. (1976). Health factors in police job stress. In W. Kroes & J. Hurrell (Eds.), *Job stress and the police officer* (pp. 73–84) (DHEW Publication No. 76-187 NIOSH). Washington, DC: U.S. Government Printing Office.

Robin, E. (1981). *The final months: A study of the lives of 134 persons who committed suicide.* New York: Oxford University Press.

Romanov, K., Hatakka, M., Keskinen, E., Laksonen, H., Kaprio, J., Rose, R., & Koskenvuo, M. (1994). Self-reported hostility and suicidal acts, accidents, and accidental deaths: A prospective study of 21,443 adults aged 25 to 29. *Psychosomatic Medicine, 56,* 328–336.

Rosenberg, M., & Pearlin, L. I. (1978). Social class and self-esteem among children and adults. *American Journal of Sociology, 84,* 53–77.

Rudestam, K. E. (1977). Physical and psychological responses to suicide in the family. *Journal of Consulting and Clinical Psychology, 45,* 162–170.

Rynearson, E. K., and McCreery, J. M. (1993). Bereavement after homicide: A synergism of trauma and loss. *Am. J. Psych., 150,* 258–261.

Sawyer, S. (1988). *Support services to surviving families of line-of-duty death.* Brandywine, Maryland: Concerns of Police Survivors, Inc., pp. 3–8.

Schwartz, J., & Schwartz, C. (1976). The personal problems of the police officer: A plea for action. In W. Kroes & J. Hurrell (Eds.), *Job stress and the police officer* (DHEW Publication No. 76-187). Washington, DC: U.S. Government Printing Office.

Selye, H. (1978). The stress of police work. *Police Stress, 1,* 1–3.

Seward, J. (1968). *Hari-kiri: Japanese ritual suicide.* Rutland, Vermont: Tuttle Publishing.

Shaffer, D., & Fisher, P. (1981). The epidemiology of suicide in children and young adolescents. *Journal of the American Academy of Child Psychiatry, 20,* 545–565.

Shneidman, E. S. (1970). Orientations toward death. In E. S. Shneidman, N. L. Farberow, & R. E. Litman (Eds.), *The psychology of suicide* (p. 7). New York: Science House.

Shneidman, E. S. (1972). Foreword. In A. C. Cain (Ed.), *Survivors of suicide* (pp. ix–xi). Springfield, IL: Charles C Thomas.

Shneidman, E. S. (1985). *Definition of suicide.* New York: Wiley, pp. 121–147.

Silverman, M. M., & Felner, R. D. (1995). The place of suicide prevention in the spectrum of intervention: Definitions of critical terms and constructs. *Suicide and Life Threatening Behavior, 25,* 10–21.

Simon, W. (1950). Attempted suicide among veterans. *Journal of Nervous and Mental Disorders, 111,* 451–468.

Skolnick, J. (1972). A sketch of the policeman's working personality. In G. F. Cole (Ed.), *Criminal justice: Law and politics* (pp. 20–42). California: Wadsworth.

Slater, J., & Depue, R. (1981). The contribution of environmental and social support to serious suicide attempts in primary depressive order. *Journal of Abnormal Psychology, 90,* 275–285.

Somodevilla, S. A. (1986). Post-shooting trauma: Reactive and proactive treatment. In J. Reese & H. Goldstein (Eds.), *Psychological services for law enforcement,* (pp. 203–205). Washington, DC: U.S. Government Printing Office.

Spielberger, C., Westberry, L., Grier, K., & Greefield, G. (1981). *The police stress survey: Sources of stress in law enforcement.* Tampa, Florida: Human Resources Institute.

Stillman, F. A. (1986). *Psychological responses of surviving spouses of public safety officers killed accidentally or feloniously in the line of duty.* Unpublished doctoral dissertation, Johns Hopkins University, Baltimore, MD.

Stillman, F. A. (1987). *Line-of-duty-deaths: Survivor and departmental responses.* Washington, DC: National Institute of Justice, pp. 1–4.

Stotland, E. (1991). The effects of police work and professional relations on health. *Journal of Criminal Justice, 19,* 371–379.

Stratton, J. G. (1978). Police stress: An overview. *Police Chief, April,* 58–62.

Stratton, J. G. (1984). Police passages. Manhattan Beach, CA: Glennon.

Stratton, J. G., Parker, D. A., & Snibbe, J. R. (1984). Posttraumatic stress: Study of police officers involved in shootings. *Psychological Reports, 55,* 127–131.

Stryker, S., & Serpe, R. T. (1982). Commitment, identity salience, and role behavior. In W. Ickes & E. S. Knowles (Eds.), *Personality, roles, and social behavior* (pp. 199–218). New York: Springer-Verlag.

Swanson, C., & Territo, L. (1983). *Police administration, structures, processes, and behaviors.* New York: MacMillan.

Symonds, M. (1970). Emotional hazards of police work. *American Journal of Psychoanalysis, 30,* 155–160.

Territo, L., & Vetter, H. (1981). Stress and police personnel. *Journal of Police Science and Administration, 9,* 95–208.

Terry, W. C. (1981). Police stress: The empirical evidence. *Journal of Police Science and Administration, 9,* 61–75, 198.

Terry, W. C. (1983). Police stress as an individual and administrative problem: Some conceptual and theoretical difficulties. *Journal of Police Science and Administration, 11,* 156–164.

Thoits, P. A. (1986). Multiple identities: Examining gender and marital differences in distress. *American Sociological Review, 51,* 259–272.

Toch, H., & Grant, J. D. (1991). *Police as problem solvers.* New York: Plenum.

Trout, D. L. (1980). The role of social isolation in suicide. *Suicide and Life-Threatening Behavior, 10,* 10–23.

Turner, J., & Beeghly, L. (1981). *The emergence of sociological theory.* Homewood, Illinois: Dorsey Press.

Turner, R. J., & Roszell, P. (1994). Psychosocial resources and the stress process. In W. R. Avison & I. H. Gotlib (Eds.), *Stress and mental health* (pp. 179–210). New York: Plenum.

Tyler, M. P., & Gifford, R. K. (1991). Field training accidents: The military unit as a recovery context. *Journal of Traumatic Stress, 4,* 233–249.

Unkovic, C., & Brown, W. (1978). The drunken cop. *Police Chief, 6,* 22–27.

Ursano, R. J., Holloway, R. C., Jones, D. R., Rodriguez, A., & Belenky, G. L. (1989). Psychiatric care in the military community: family and military stressors. *Hosp. & Comm. Psych., 40,* 1284–1289.

Van Raalte, R. C. (1979). Alcohol as a problem among police officers. *Police Chief, 44,* 38–40.

Vena, J. E., Violanti, J. M., Marshall, J. R., & Fiedler, F. (1986). Mortality of a municipal worker cohort III: Police officers. *Journal of Industrial Medicine, 10,* 383–397.

Violanti, J. M. (1978). Police stress: A definition. *Police Stress, 1,* 4–5.

Violanti, J. M. (1981). *Police stress and coping: An organizational analysis.* Unpublished doctoral dissertation, State University of New York at Buffalo, Buffalo, NY.

Violanti, A. W. (1983). For some veterans, the war still rages on. *Buffalo News,* September 13, C2.

Violanti, J. M., Marshall, J. R., & Howe, B. (1983). Police occupational demands, psychological distress, and the coping function of alcohol. *Journal of Occupational Medicine, 25,* 455–458.

Violanti, J. M. (1984). Police suicide: On the rise. *New York Trooper, 1,* 18–19.

Violanti, J. M. (1986). Shift work may be hazardous to your health. *New York Trooper, 3,* 7–10.

Violanti, J. M., Vena, J. E., & Marshall, J. R. (1986). Disease risk and mortality among police officers. *Journal of Police Science and Administration, 14,* 17–23.

Violanti, J. M. (1990). Post-trauma vulnerability: A proposed model. In J. T. Reese, J. M. Horn, & C. Dunning (Eds.), *Critical incidents in policing.* (pp. 503–510). Washington, DC: U.S. Government Printing.

Violanti, J. M. (1992). *Police retirement: The impact of change* (pp. 75–81). Springfield, Illinois: Charles C Thomas.

Violanti, J. M. (1993a). Coping in a high stress police environment. *Journal of Social Psychology,* 717–730.

Violanti, J. M. (1993b). High stress police training: What does it teach police recruits? *Journal of Criminal Justice, 21,* 411–417.

Violanti, J. M., & Aron, F. (1994). Ranking police stressors. *Psychological Reports, 75,* 824–826.

Violanti, J. M. (1994). The mystery within: Explaining police suicide. *FBI Law Enforcement Bulletin, 64,* 19–23.

Violanti, J. M. (1995). Survivor's trauma and departmental response following deaths of police officers. *Psychological Reports, 77,* 611–615.

Violanti, J. M., & Vena, J. E. *Epidemiology of police suicide.* Research in progress, NIMH grant MH47091-02.

Violanti, J. M., Vena, J. E., Marshall, J. R., & Petralia, S. (in press). A comparative evaluation of police suicide rate validity. *Suicide and Life-Threatening Behavior.*

Violanti, J. M., Vena, J. E., & Marshall, J. R. (in press). Suicides, homicides, and accidental death: A comparative risk assessment of police officers and municipal workers. *Am. Journal of Industrial Medicine.*

Violanti, J. M. (in press). Trauma stress and police work. In D. Paton & J. Violanti (Eds.), *Traumatic stress in critical occupations.* Springfield, IL: Charles C Thomas.

Whitis, P. R. (1972). The legacy of a child's suicide. In A. C. Cain (Ed.), *Survivors of suicide* (pp. 155–166). Springfield, IL: Charles C Thomas.

Williams, C. (1987). Peacetime combat: Treating and preventing delayed stress reactions in police officers. In T. Williams (Ed.), *Post-traumatic stress disorders: A handbook for clinicians* (pp. 267–292). Cincinnati, Ohio: Disabled American Veterans.

AUTHOR INDEX

A

Abernathy, C.B., 87, 92
Adam, K.S., 59, 67, 91
Aldridge, D., 26, 91
Allen, S., 36, 53, 59, 91
Alpert, G.P., 32, 91
Amick-McMullin, A., 85, 91
Angell, J., 31, 93
Arato, M., 45, 91
Argyle, M., 87, 91
Arnone, H.C., 85, 91
Aron, F.H., 31, 32, 34, 85, 91, 101
Asgard, U., 46, 91
Aussant, G., 45, 52, 91
Aveline, M.O., 37, 93
Avison, W.R., 100

B

Baechler, J., 57, 91
Bard, M., 85, 91
Banton, J.G., 44, 45, 95
Bargagli, A., 93
Barraclough, B.M., 26, 28, 91, 94
Bayley, D.H., 42, 91
Beeghly, L., 72, 100
Beehr, T., 81, 92
Belenky, G.L., 100
Beutler, L.E., 46, 92
Binder, A., 41, 42, 93
Blumberg, M., 32, 95
Blumenthal, S.J., 91
Bonafacio, P., 33, 36, 57, 58, 68, 92
Borgia, P., 93
Boyle, C., 28, 97
Braverman, M., 78, 92
Brown, M.K., 66, 92
Brown, W., 46, 100

Browning, J.H., 45, 80, 92
Brzeczak, 14, 46
Bullman, T.A., 39, 93
Burdo, H., 28, 95
Burger, J.M., 36, 75, 92
Burns, L., 36, 75, 92

C

Cain, A.C., 99, 101
Calhoun, L.G., 87, 92
Campbell, T., 70, 72, 92
Carroll, E.M., 37, 93
Checkoway, H., 24, 92
Cicourel, A., 26, 28, 95
Cohen, D., 96
Cole, G.F., 99
Conroy, R.W., 67, 92
Coyne, J., 81, 92
Crawford-Brown, D.J., 24, 92
Cronin, T.J., 9, 10, 16, 22, 26, 46, 92
Curphey, T., 28, 96
Curran, P.S., 26, 92

D

Danieli, Y., 33, 85, 92
Danto, B.L., 15, 16, 22, 33, 36, 45, 52, 87, 88, 92, 93
Dash, J., 26, 93
David, Jonathan, 77
DeAngelis, T., 81, 93
Demeter, E., 45, 91
Depue, R., 52, 99
DiPietro, A., 93
Dollinger, S.J., 37, 75, 94
Douglas, J., 26, 28, 93
Downey, G., 81, 92
Dubner, J.S., 96

103

Dunham, R.G., 32, 91
Durkheim, E., 55, 69, 72, 93

E

Eisdorfer, C., 968
Eisenberg, T., 85, 93
Elkind, D., 36, 93
Ellison, K., 31, 93
Etzion, D., 81, 93

F

Farberow, N.L., 28, 39, 40, 53, 93, 96, 99
Fell, R., 25, 98
Felner, R.D., 78, 99
Fenley, M.A., 97
Fiedler, F., 17, 25, 28, 100
Figley, C.R., 88, 91, 93, 94
Finlay, R.J., 26, 92
Fisher, P., 43, 99
Fligner, C., 44, 45, 95
Forastiere, F., 25, 93
Fowler, R.C., 45, 98
Fowlie, D.G., 37, 93
Foy, D.W., 37, 93
Francisco, J., 44, 45, 49
Freud, Sigmund, 54, 55
Frey-Wouters, E., 38, 96
Fridell, L.A., 41, 42, 93
Friedman, Paul, vii, 32, 33, 45, 51, 52, 55, 93
Frye, J., 37, 93
Furnham, A., 87, 91

G

Gaines, L., 31, 93
Gallops, M.S., 38, 96
Gaska, C.W., 47, 83, 94
Gecas, V., 61, 94
Genz, J., 31, 93
Gibbs, J.P., 26, 56, 94
Giddens, A., 72, 94
Gifford, 85
Gleser, G.C., 85, 94
Goldstein, H., 91, 97, 99
Gotlib, I.H., 100
Grace, M.C., 85, 94
Graf, F., 32, 94

Graham, J.A., 87, 91
Grant, J.D., 41, 100
Green, B.L., 85, 94
Greenfield, G., 31, 99
Greening, L., 37, 75, 94
Grier, K., 31, 99
Gross, E., 64, 94
Guralnick, L., 21, 24, 94

H

Haas, A.P., 39, 94
Hackman, B.B., 44, 45, 95
Hagedorn, R., 25, 44, 51, 96
Hageman, M., 33, 94
Harris, R.N., 65, 94
Hatakka, M., 46, 51, 98
Hauser, M.J., 86, 94
Hearst, N., 39, 94
Heiman, M.F., 14, 15, 25, 36, 52, 56, 94
Hendin, H., 39, 94
Henry, A., 54, 94
Hitz, D., 46, 94
Holding, T.A., 28, 94
Holloway, R.C., 100
Horn, J.M., 33, 100
Hovanitz, C.A., 41, 95
Howe, B., 41, 100
Hulley, S.B., 94
Hurrell, J.J., Jr., 93, 95, 98

I

Ickes, W., 99
Ivanoff, A., 18, 22, 44, 67, 77, 78, 80, 81, 82, 95
Ivanoff, I., 76, 77, 78, 95

J

Jacobson, G.F., 67, 95
Janik, J., 52, 95
Jones, D.R., 100
Josephson, R.L., 26, 95

K

Kamerman, J., 34, 85, 95
Kang, H.K., 39, 93
Kappeler, V.E., 32, 95

SUBJECT INDEX